SOLVE YOUR HORSE AND PONY PROBLEMS

Karen Bush & Sarah Viccars

with illustrations by Christine Bousfield

RIGHT WAY

CONTENTS

For the real
Stephanie Birchall
with love

Equestrian titles in our low-price Paperfront series

Horsekeepers Encyclopedia
Right Way To Keep Ponies
Buying & Fitting Saddlery
Right Way To Ride A Horse
Practical Horsemanship

Introduction

Horse or pony keeping is not always the bed of roses imagined; animals can hardly ever be relied upon to behave predictably, or even in the manner described in so many horsy books.

Horsekeeping, therefore, is seldom as straightforward as it at first seems, whether for the new owner, or for one who is more knowledgeable. This book does not pretend to solve all the problems which may possibly occur, nor does it claim to have found all of the solutions to those which are mentioned. However it tries to highlight the commonest practical problems which people encounter, but which are overlooked by many books, and to give sound advice on coping and dealing with them.

It should also be of some interest to those who have not yet acquired a horse or pony, as plenty of information of interest to the casual, or "weekend" rider has also been included.

1

To Buy or not to Buy?

Q. I am considering taking a pony on loan; I know both the owner and pony quite well, but nevertheless, are there any precautions I should take?

A.   Loaning a pony can be a mutually agreeable arrangement for both the owner and the loanee; it may be up for loan for a number of reasons, ranging from the owner having outgrown it, but not wishing to part with it entirely, or due to lack of time or finances. However, there can be a number of catches for the unwary. A suitable horse or pony for loan may be heard of by word of mouth, or through adverts in the 'Pets and Livestock' columns of local newspapers, or in the 'For Loan' sections of most horsy magazines. Having found an animal which sounds as though it may be suitable, both parties would then be well advised to proceed with caution. From the loanee's point of view, the same priorities must be taken into account as when actually considering purchase. The initial outlay of buying may have been avoided, but thereafter the horse or pony will still need feeding, shoeing, regular veterinary attention, possibly stabling, and everyday care, which can still be a considerable financial drain. Suitable facilities must also be available where the animal can be kept, especially as the owner will probably wish to see the place in order to set his mind at rest, before finally agreeing to a loan. The pony should be ridden by the prospective loanee when going to see it, and if possible, ridden out on the roads too in order to check its reliability in traffic. The owner will also want to know something about the loanee's capability and general level of knowledge about caring for a horse or pony properly, and is likely to ask a few questions about the sort of routine and exercise it is likely to receive, plus the activities for which it will be used. In return, the loanee must not only answer these questions honestly but enquire himself as to the age and veterinary history of the animal, and any conditions which may be attached, such as restrictions of use, and whether regular visits by the owner, with the opportunity of an occasional ride are expected. Before agreeing to a more final and binding contract, the animal should also be 'vetted' and checked by a veterinary surgeon for any physical defects which might prove to be a problem in the future. Which party pays for this service will have to be agreed upon; it is usually assumed that the loanee will, but the owner may agree to meet some of the costs. Should the results of the vetting prove satisfactory, then a contract between both parties should be drawn up by a solicitor. This should include the following points, which will require some discussion to reach a fair agreement:

Shoeing: how frequently this will be, and who is responsible for the bills (normally the loanee).

Veterinary bills: the loanee is normally responsible for all of these, although the owner may agree to pay part or all, of the bills incurred for regular 'flu and tetanus injections.

Insurance: the horse or pony should be insured (and the tack as well); it may be agreed to split the amount since this is also in the owner's interest – or the loanee may have to agree to pay all of it.

Saddlery: a list should be made of all items of saddlery, horse clothing, grooming kit and so forth, which will accompany the animal. In the event of anything becoming lost or broken, the loanee is normally held responsible for replacement or repair. Tack should be carefully examined beforehand, since if it is very old and worn it will not only prove unsafe to use, but may cost the loanee a considerable amount.

Feed bills and rent: these are entirely the loanee's responsibility. The location the horse or pony is to be kept at should be stated, and the owner kept informed as to any changes.

Use of horse/pony: The activities it is allowed to be used for should be listed, since the owner may be anxious that it not take part in events where it is more likely to injure itself, such as hunting, or cross country competitions. A mention could also be made here as to whether any other people, other than the loanee, are to be allowed to ride it.

Length of loan: Initially this is best kept to a fairly short period, say for two months, after which, if the loan is working out satisfactorily, it could be renewed for a longer period after which the contract could again be renewed, reviewed, or terminated if wished.

Terms of notice for return: To be fair to both parties, this should also be agreed upon, so that the owner does not suddenly find a horse or pony returned, with no opportunity of organising somewhere to keep it, or alternatively, so that the loanee does not suddenly find it whisked away having perhaps already made plans for future activities. A period of about a month is usually satisfactory. Provision should also be made for the return of the animal should it become incurably lame, or affected in some way as to make it impossible for the loanee to ride it again. Two copies of the contract, both signed by owner and by the loanee should be made, and a copy kept by each. It may seem overcautious going to such lengths, but even good friends have been known to fall out over less!

Q. My daughter has been riding for several years now, and helps out at the local riding stables every weekend, and several evenings during the week as well. Since she is so keen, and it is obviously not just a passing phase, I should like to buy her a pony. Where is the best place to buy from, and what breed would be best?

A.   Auctions should most definitely be avoided, as it is impossible for the inexperienced to pick out something suitable – even the experts have been known to make mistakes! You could try a reputable local dealer, but you should sound out a few opinions in your area first. Most dealers are not 'con men' as they are frequently portrayed to be, and cannot afford to risk their reputation, but they are nevertheless in business to make money, and some are perhaps a little less scrupulous than they should be. Your daughter is also far less likely to get such a good opportunity of really trying out a suitable pony; your best bet is probably to look through adverts in local newspapers, and in the 'For Sale' columns of horsy magazines. You could also enquire at the riding school where she helps out, as they may well have heard of something which would be right for her. You should enlist their advice and assistance if available. Having found one or two 'possibles' ask an instructor who is familiar with your daughter's riding capabilities to come and have a look with you both. You will probably need to pay him or her for their time, but it can be very helpful in trying to make a sensible choice. When looking around for a pony, stick to the area locally if possible, since you will also be able to find out more easily about its reputation, and whether it really is the genuine animal that it seemed when you saw it. As far as breed is concerned, unless your daughter has specifically set her heart on showing, it is relatively unimportant. It is more to the point that it is of the right size, build and temperament for her to be comfortable with and able to handle confidently, and capable of performing adequately at whatever activities she will want to try her hand at.

Q.   I realise that keeping a horse is likely to prove expensive – but what sort of bills am I going to have to consider if I do go ahead and purchase one?

A.   There are plenty of 'hidden' expenses to consider when buying a horse or pony. Firstly, you will need to pay for its accommodation; a weekly field rent, which may cost extra if stabling is required in addtion. In built up arcas cspecially, where grazing is often at a premium, it may sometimes be a good idea to rent some grazing even before you have actually bought a horse or pony, rather than risk losing a vacancy and not being able to find another when you really need it.   On top of this, in the winter you will need to pay for hay (unless it is included in the field rent) and if stabled.for all or part of the time, for bedding as well. Therè will also be bills for concentrate feeds; you can work out how much these will roughly cost, plus the price of bedding, if you ask for a price list from your local feed merchant. You may need to buy new saddlery, and throughout the year it will nccd to be kept clean and repaired. Even if no accidents occur, the vet will need to make two yearly visits, for teeth rasping and to administer 'flu and tetanus injections. If an insurance policy is taken out, you should find it possible to insure against veterinary bills over certain amounts, which will help you out in a crisis. All the equipment necessary to care for your horse properly will need to be bought, including grooming kit, rugs, stable equipment and mucking out tools. On top of all this, any horse or pony you buy will need to be wormed every six to eight weeks, shod every four to six weeks, and you may find that you are also liable for a certain amount of stable and field maintenance. Financial considerations aside, you will also need to find plenty of time to look after it!

Q.   Having found a suitable pony, should I get someone to look it over before buying it? It looks all right to me.

A.   Ask your local horse vet to come and vet the pony at a time convenient for the owners. If possible, be present yourself so that you can see all that goes on, and so the vet can explain any peculiarities and the effect they are likely to have. 'Vetting' consists of a really thorough examination, during which the animal is examined physically for any problems, ranging from defective eyesight, to unusual lumps and bumps, and a sound heart. A description is also made of him. He will also be trotted up so that the vet can check that he does not appear to be lame,

Fig. 1. Horse being trotted up for a vet.

and finally will need to be galloped and cantered in tight circles so that he can test the wind. You will also be asked for what purposes you intend to use him, and the vet will finally produce a certificate, all being well, stating that he is sound for the purposes you want to use him for. Should the pony fail, do not disregard the vet's opinion, thinking that you know best, however disappointed you may be. Should something go wrong after purchase in such a case, you will not be able to return the animal, and may be faced with hefty veterinary bills.

Q. I am considering buying my first horse – what sort of things should I take into consideration?

A.   Make a list of your priorities so that you have a clear idea of what you are looking for – there is no point in wasting either your own (or other people's) time. Don't be too inflexible either, or your search for perfection could last you a lifetime!

First of all, consider your finances; this will limit the amount you are able to spend, and halve the number of adverts which you have to look through. Money must also be considered when deciding what type of horse you want; an animal capable of living outdoors all the year round will obviously work out much cheaper to keep than one which needs stabling. It will also be less demanding on your time (although it will still need checking each day) and will be able to exercise itself should you be unable to ride for some reason.

Something fairly tough, preferably with native blood for hardiness, and already used to living out, would be most suitable in this instance, unless you have both the time and the money for an animal which is more finely bred and requires coddling. Decide on the height you would be comfortable with – and the build necessary. A 15 hh horse may be the right height for you, but may not necessarily be of a sturdy enough build to cope with your weight comfortably if you are fairly solid. In such cases, if you want to stick with that height, you will need to look around for something quite chunky and cobby. On the other hand, if you are of a slender build, something of the same height, but rather narrower and less strong will be more suitable if you are to remain in control. Unless you have any really strong dislikes, colour or sex should not play a part in your choice; however, temperament and ability should. You do need to be totally honest with yourself about your capabilities, and stick to something which you know you will be safe on, unless you are a very confident and able rider ready for something more advanced. If the animal is to become a companion with whom you will wish to spend some time, then a nice nature is also important. One that snaps and kicks all the time is not very pleasant to handle, although these vices might be overlooked in a horse bought purely for its ability in competition. Consider also the activities for which you will want to use it; a good Riding Club horse or Pony Club pony must have reasonably good conformation if it is to be at all successful and remain sound. Rather less good conformation can be tolerated to a degree if the animal will not be expected to exert itself much more than for a quiet hack around the block.

However, do avoid buying anything which suffers from a serious defect, or a minor one which is likely to become progressively worse. When trying out any horse or pony, give it a fair trial – ask if you can tack it up yourself, and having seen it ridden for you, put it thoroughly through all of its paces on

Fig. 2. A horse with a fair conformation.

both reins, and possibly pop it over a small jump too. Ask if you can see it ridden on the roads – even if the owner is reluctant to allow you to do this. Unless there is some serious problem he/she should not object to taking it out whilst you follow on foot to observe its reactions. Should you feel that this is just the animal for you, make an appointment to see it once again the following day, or a few days later, so that you do not make a hurried decision in the heat of the moment. Consider it all carefully, and do not allow yourself to be pushed into anything, or you may regret it later.

Q.   I am considering buying my first horse – should I ask for a contract of sale, and what should be included?

A.   Someone who is selling a horse or pony does not have to agree to sign a contract of sale. But it does have advantages. Providing it is reasonable in its specifications, and is fair to both parties and protects them, then at least both vendor and purchaser know what each expects of the other as a result of the transaction. If a vendor refuses to be bound by a contract, then it should certainly raise a few suspicions in the mind of the purchaser, and great care should be taken.

The names of both vendor and purchaser, with their addresses, should be included in the contract, together with the sum agreed for the animal, which should be named and briefly described. The activities for which the horse is warranted sound should be stated, plus any exceptions, vices or unsoundnesses. A length of time (usually not exceeding seven days) should be stated for the return of the horse if it is found not to comply with the description; and saying that it should be accompanied by a signed certificate from a qualified veterinary surgeon specifying in what respect(s) the horse fails to comply. In the event of a dispute, a vet is to be agreed upon by both parties, whose decision is binding. Two copies of the contract should be made, dated and signed by both vendor and purchaser, and a copy kept by each. A solicitor can help with the wording; but it is inadvisable to sign any contract unless the animal has been vetted first.

2

Equitation – Flatwork

Q.   I've been riding for some time now, but I still get saddle sore. Is this because I'm not sitting properly? Or could it be due to the saddle?

A.   There are several possibilities here, one of which could be that the saddle is very hard – riding school saddles are not exactly notorious for their comfort for example! Neither are rigid tree saddles as luxurious as spring tree ones; if you want to know which it is, a spring tree saddle will be stamped to that effect on the panel, beneath the flap. The problem could also be partly due to your build – if you are thin you might try using a seatsaver made of sheepskin or synthetic fleece to provide a little more padding for the nether regions. These are also pleasantly warm during the winter months – and, if you do not wish to go to the expense of buying one, can easily be made yourself from offcuts. The way in which you are sitting is another pos-

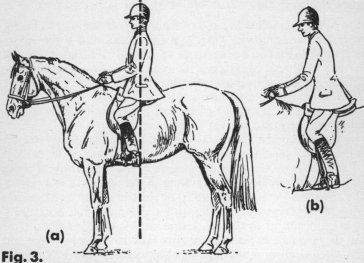

Fig. 3.
(a) Rider in the correct position.
(b) Rider in an incorrect position.

sibility; if you tip forward and perch in the saddle rather than sitting squarely on your seat bones, you are also likely to become sore. Correct your position if you think that could be the cause – ask a friend, or better still, your instructor, to comment on it, and ways in which to improve.

Q.   I ride as a hobby, and enjoy looking after my own horse, finding that together with riding him, it is a really enjoyable way of keeping fit. The trouble is, it does seem to be making my muscles rather large and prominent, and I dislike looking so unfeminine.

A.   Unfortunately, looking after horses is a job which requires physical exertion, and the toning up and development of the muscles from doing so is an occupational hazard. The only solution is to put the horse on full livery, so that someone else looks after it and takes on all the heavier jobs such as mucking out, and carrying bales of bedding around, which are building up your muscles.

Q.   My pony is stabled all the time, and is very fresh and difficult to handle when I ride him. He fidgets and jogs everywhere even when I only want him to walk, and so is very tiring. Are there some schooling aids which will make him more obedient?

A.   This pony is less in need of schooling aids than of a change in stable management. Turn him out for at least a few hours every day so that he has a chance to unwind mentally, and work off any freshness. Make sure that you are not overfeeding him for the amount of exercise you give him, and reduce or cut out altogether any cereals which could cause him to get even more excitable. Have a saddler check the fit of his tack too, so you know that he is not merely reacting to pain.

   You might find it beneficial to spend some time quietly school-ing at home, teaching him to accept and respond to the contact of your leg, rather than evading it by rushing away. Taking your legs off his sides, and pulling at the reins will only make the situation worse, as he will pull back in return and become uptight. When you are riding with a group of other horses, try and keep him at the front, either on his own, or abreast of another person, so that he does not feel that he is in a race and has to chase after a tail in front of him. Keep your legs quietly in contact with his sides, to keep him active and using his hind quarters, so that he takes up a positive contact with the bit.

Q. Whenever my pony is standing still, she paws continually at the ground with a front foot — how do I stop her?

A.   This sounds like a bad habit that she has been allowed to get into. It may spring from impatience to be on the move again, but is nevertheless very ill-mannered. It could be potentially dangerous if someone is standing nearby. Each time she does this, scold her, and give her a sharp smack with your stick on the shoulder of the offending leg. When she does stand quietly, reward her with a pat and a kind word. It may take a little while to correct the habit, but provided you are firm and persevere, she should learn that it is far more pleasant to behave herself.

Q. I've just bought a four year old gelding, but he seems to be terribly clumsy and wobbly, although in other respects he is good natured and well behaved. Is this a physical defect, or will it get better after a while?

A.   You should certainly call your vet if you think that there is any physical problem causing lack of balance and co-ordination, but it sounds more likely that it is simply due to his youth A four year old is not the best balanced animal in the world, and has to learn how to readjust his balance to cope with the unaccustomed weight of a rider in the saddle. With schooling and time, his co-ordination and strength should improve, so that you have a more manoeuvrable and balanced ride. Until this happens, you should use brushing boots on him so that he does not injure himself by moving a little awkwardly.

Q. My pony won't lead. He hangs back all the time so that I have to drag him along, and if he doesn't feel like going somewhere he just digs his heels in and stands still.

A.   Try carrying a short stick with you, holding it in your left hand with the end of the lead rope or reins. Stand midway between your pony's eye and shoulder, and firmly give the command to 'walk on'. If he won't oblige, bring the stick around behind your back, and give him a sharp smack with it in the girth region. This should have the effect of making him go forward; walk on beside him, encouraging with your voice and stick if necessary. Do not get in front of his eye, or start tugging at him, as it is more likely to create, rather than overcome resistance.

Fig. 4. How to encourage a reluctant pony to lead.

Q. I have a problem with my boots when riding. I cannot afford made-to-measure leather boots, but the rubber off-the-peg variety flap around my calves. When I ride without stirrups, they continually slide down, and I have to keep stopping in order to pull them back up. Is there anything I can do about this?

A. A number of brands of rubber riding boots are now made in different calf width fittings, as well as foot sizes, so it is worth trying on several types to find the ones which are the best fit. In the summer, jodhpur boots provide a cooler alternative to long boots, and you will not have the same problem. In the winter, when you will wish to wear your long boots, wear an extra pair of thick socks inside. If the foot of the boot is not large enough to allow room for this, just put on a pair of leg-warmers instead. You could also stitch a loop of leather into the top of the back seam of the boots, through which you can thread spur, or boot straps, which are then buckled around your legs.

Q. How can I tell when my horse is on the correct canter lead? I am never really sure – is it that important anyway?

A. Your horse should appear to be taking longer strides with his inside foreleg, ie. the one that is to the inside of the bends he is taking, when he is on the correct canter lead. This enables him to stay better balanced on turns. Try running a small circle yourself, on your own two feet taking first short strides, and then long strides, with your inside leg, and you will soon appreciate the difference that it makes to him in being able to keep his balance. With practice you will eventually be able to feel which leg he is leading (taking longer strides) with, but it will take a little time and perseverance to acquire the knack. Whenever you ask for canter, first of all try and decide whether it is the correct leg or not, and then check by glancing downwards at the shoulders. Do not actually lean over to one side, or you will unbalance your horse, and if you are in a showing or dressage competition, it looks very obvious and unprofessional. Simply glance down – the shoulder will swing further forward on the side to which the foreleg is leading. If on the wrong leg for the direction you are going, trot or walk and ask again.

Q. I am rather short, and have a lot of trouble mounting because of this. It is very embarrassing having to struggle on board in front of other people, and I dread having to dismount for any reason when I am out hacking.

A.   It is possible to buy extending stirrup leathers, which will

Fig. 5. Giving someone a leg up.

help solve your problems whilst out hacking, should you need to dismount. If someone is around, ask for a leg up – this is far better than having to heave yourself on board, which can damage the horse's back or saddle. Failing this, make a mounting block at home; one can be made quite easily from a few breeze blocks and cement. When away from home, you can always make use of gates and logs from which to mount if you really get stuck. If you are a little overweight, slimming down can help. Unless you have a specific physical problem limiting your suppleness, you can limber up a little by using the following dismounted exercise. Put one foot on the seat of a chair placed in front of you. Then turn the foot which is on the ground so that it is at right angles to the chair, and slowly lean forward

Fig. 6. A leg stretching exercise.

so that your weight moves forward over the raised leg. Repeat it with the other leg so that you do not become one sided when riding.

Q.   I seem to have an awful lot of trouble controlling my feet. They seem to keep sliding forwards, and my feet slip right through the irons, or I lose them altogether, no matter how hard I try to keep the iron on the ball of my foot. How can I keep them in the right place?

A.   Most of this problem stems from stiffness, which prevents you from acquiring a deeper seat. Instead of sitting into the saddle and being able to use your legs independently, you are probably locking your joints, gripping with your knees, and pushing onto your toes.

When you first mount, sit in the centre of the saddle, with your feet free of the stirrup irons. Lift both legs slightly away to each side, holding the front arch of the saddle to help you keep your balance, and then settle them back into the correct position. This should be with your ankle and knee joints flexed so that the knees turn slightly away from the saddle flap, and so that when you look downwards, you cannot see the toes of each foot peeping past the front of the kneecaps. Place your feet carefully back in the stirrup irons, and if your legs are in the right place, the leathers should hang down vertically from the stirrup bars.

Try not to ride with your stirrup irons too long, or you will aggravate, not improve, the situation. It is often better to start off with slightly shorter stirrups and slowly let them down as you become more supple and able to sit deeper into the saddle. Allow your ankle joints to relax, and the heel to sink downwards, so that your foot does not slip through the iron – but do not force the heel down so hard that the lower leg shoots forward. A pair of rubber treads fitted to the irons will also reduce the problem of your feet slipping through them. If possible, you should also try and get a few lessons; it always helps to have constructive criticism from someone on the ground who can see exactly what is going wrong and offer advice on correcting it.

Q. I have just started riding, and am having a lot of trouble with the rising trot. I can manage it for a little while, but then I find that I lose my balance. Am I doing something wrong?

A.   This is a very common problem amongst novice riders, but with time and practice it will improve, so that after a while you will wonder what all the fuss was about! It is best if you can practise rising trot on a horse with a fairly active gait, and which also moves with a reasonably constant tempo. If it is constantly stopping and starting, then you may have trouble picking up the rhythm and falling into the movement. Once you have acquired more co-ordination, you will find it easier to use your legs to keep this type going, but for the moment, you need something which will keep going at a reasonable speed without too much encouragement. Try and allow the bouncy movement of the horse's back to do some of the work for you. Incline your upper body slightly forwards, and allow your hips to be pushed in an upwards and forwards direction as you feel the horse's back begin to throw your seat in the air. Then gently allow your seat to sink down, and start again. A good exercise to practise is to hover with your seat raised slightly out of the saddle. You will probably need to take a handful of mane so

Fig. 7. A hovering exercise.

that you can keep your balance more easily. Flex your ankles and knees so they work as shock absorbers, and try to find a position where you are sufficiently balanced as not to need to hang onto the mane too tightly. Maintain this position for a few strides, and then continue in the 'up – down' rising movement, and then repeat. When you have your lessons with your instructor, discuss your problem, as there are plenty of other things which would also help.

Q.   I seem to have trouble finding the right length of stirrup How long should it be?

A.   The length of stirrup depends on both the activity you are engaged in, and your standard of riding. Generally speaking, when working on the flat, you should ride with as long a stirrup as possible, so that as much of your leg as possible is in contact with the horse's sides. When jumping, your stirrups will need to be shortened, by perhaps as much as three or four holes to allow you to go forward with him over a jump. If you are galloping, a length somewhere between these two is about right to enable you to raise your seat from the saddle in order to stay forward over the centre of gravity and free the horse's back. The other factor affecting the length of stirrup you ride with is your standard of riding; the more advanced you are, the longer the stirrup you will be able to cope with. More novice riders need slightly shorter stirrups, particularly when learning to do the rising trot. To gauge your approximate length of stirrup before mounting, place the knuckle of one hand on the stirrup bar, and lift the stirrup iron up beneath your armpit; the leather should lie along the length of your arm. Once actually

Fig. 8. Checking the length of stirrup leathers.

mounted, you may need to adjust this slightly, either longer or shorter to suit.

Q. My horse is very nappy; she does not like to leave other horses, which can create problems when I want to go out my own. Should I smack her, or try and coax her – I don't want to spoil her by doing the wrong thing.

A.   Nappiness is quite common in young horses, and is a habit that should be nipped in the bud before it becomes more established and difficult to correct. Even a normally well-behaved horse, however, can become particularly attached to another, and can be reluctant to leave it. A weak and ineffective rider can encourage a horse to take advantage of the situation. Whatever you do though, you should not dismount and lead her, but rather try and ride through the problem instead. Do not tip

forwards, but sit up straight, or if necessary, with the upper
body slightly behind the vertical to give you more push. Use
your legs firmly, and keep a proper rein contact; when she
begins to dig her heels in, give her a couple of sharp smacks
with a stick to drive her on. Use your voice too and persevere
until she obeys you. If you adopt these strong tactics, she will
eventually give in. Some horses try to whip round and turn
back, and if you are not quick enough to stop this from happening, you should turn her in a couple of short circles, and then
point her back in the direction you wish to go, still urging her
strongly onwards. When riding in company, instead of always
following, ride alongside someone. Gradually push her on until
you are taking the lead, and be ready to get after her the instant
you feel any reluctance. Hesitation will be interpreted as weak-
ness on your part. Try to avoid doing things which will encourage
nappiness – not just following others, but habits such as always
cantering towards the field gate. When out hacking, never turn
and retrace your footsteps, but try and find a circular route
instead.

*Q.   I only ride once a week, at a local riding school. Each time
I start the lesson, I find I am so stiff that it takes me a long time
to loosen off enough to gain any real benefit. Are there any
exercises I could do which will help me to stay supple during the
rest of the week when I am unable to ride?*

A.   It can be really helpful for the occasional rider to use some
dismounted exercises in between lessons. It will reduce the
amount of time taken loosening off when first getting back in
the saddle, and you will be less likely to ache as much the next
day. They need not take up a great deal of time; indeed many
can easily be worked in around household chores, whilst sitting
at an office desk, or even whilst watching the television. They
could also be used as a means of limbering up just prior to a
lesson. Here are a few exercises:

Head rolling: Excellent for relaxing tension in the neck. Allow
the head to tilt forwards so that the chin rests on the chest, and
gently and slowly roll the head from side to side.

Shoulder shrug: Hunch both the shoulders up beneath the ears,
breathing inwards at the same time. Then roll the shoulders
back and downwards, breathing out again.

Arm circling: Slowly circle each arm in turn through a backwards circle, stretching up through the ribcage as the arm moves above the head, and rolling the shoulders back and downwards as the arms come to rest by the side of the body.

Elbow push: Hold both arms, elbows bent and finger tips lightly touching, in front of the rib cage at chest height. Push both elbows backwards as far as they will go, keeping the arms parallel to the ground.

Wrist suppling: Rotate the wrist joints. Let the hands and fingers relax downwards, and gently shake them up and down and also sideways, trying to keep the rest of the forearm fairly steady.

Waist: Hold both arms out to the sides at shoulder height, with the palms uppermost. Swing them around the body, rotating from the waist. Keep the arms in a straight line with each other. Keep the feet spread slightly apart. Then reach down and touch each foot in turn with the fingers of the opposite hand. After that, allow the arms to hang by the sides, and reach down the side of each leg in turn, as far as possible, by inclining the body over in that direction.

Thigh stretch: Place one foot on a chair placed just in front. Turn the foot on the ground so that it is at right angles to the chair. Then lean forward so that your weight moves forwards over the raised knee.

Ankle circling: Whilst sitting down, rotate the ankle joints in both directions.

Lower legs: Stand at arms length from a wall, resting the palms of each hand on its surface. Bend the elbows so that the body inclines forward, keeping the heels flat on the floor. Then push the body away again, until upright once more.

These exercises are on the whole, more beneficial when performed slowly, and if there are any physical disabilities, then a doctor should also be consulted first before attempting them. Attention should also be paid to normal posture, making an effort not to slouch or round the shoulders. It is also best to avoid crossing the legs, as this can lead to uneven muscular development, and crookedness when riding.

Q. My horse will never canter on the correct leg on the left rein. How can I make him do it properly?

A. There may be a number of reasons why your horse is having problems. If he has been checked over and there are no physical causes, then you will have to put in some extra work on his schooling to try and correct it. Always ask for the canter in a place where his balance is such as to predispose him to striking off correctly – either on a circle or in a corner, when you have established a correct bend to the inside. Throughout the entire transition you will have to maintain this bend. Stiff horses will frequently try and evade it if they are allowed, so you may need to be very firm and positive. Most will try to avoid cantering on the difficult lead by bending to the outside, propping weight onto the inside shoulder, and swinging the quarters outwards. All your aids need to be directed at preventing this. Keep the outside leg drawn firmly backwards to control

Fig. 9. The canter sequence, with the right 'off' fore leading.

the quarters, and raise the inside hand a little to help maintain bend and prevent the weight from being dropped onto the inside shoulder. If you are able to, even push the quarters inwards a little bit, so that the outside hindleg (the first one to push off into canter) is really engaged strongly. Each time you get a wrong transition, stop and try again. It may take time, but persevere, rewarding your horse with a pat and plenty of praise when he gets it right, and you will soon find he becomes more consistent.

Q.   My pony is rather lazy, and never goes forward into another pace when I want him to. He shuffles along a bit faster, and eventually breaks into the pace — but it isn't really the instant response to my leg signals that I would like!

A.   Buy a long schooling whip to reinforce your leg signals. Get him as active as possible in each gait; if his quarters are engaged well underneath him, he will be better prepared to spring forwards into the next one. Although this means that you will need to use plenty of leg, try to avoid being punishing with them, or else his sides will grow numb after a while, and he will stop taking any notice of you at all. If you find that you do not get enough response when you apply your legs, rather than kicking, use them again and at the same time give him a little flick with the stick just behind your calf. Practise riding lots of transitions one after the other to keep him on his toes and alert. Use small circles (between 10 and 15 metres diameter) to get him using his back end more.

Q.   Each time I ask for canter, my horse just rushes off, and can often be quite difficult to stop again. Should I persevere, or keep canter work to the minimum so that he doesn't get worked up?

A.   It is best to spend more time working on the canter, so that it becomes accepted as work, rather than as a good excuse for naughtiness or a show of temperament. Be careful not to be over-severe with the leg aids, and think of the best ways in which to approach the problem. Cantering for long periods of time, for example, will give him the chance to take charge, so canter work is best divided into relatively short periods, doing other work in between. A good exercise would be to set yourself a certain number of strides in each gait, eg ten strides trot, ten strides canter, ten strides trot, and so on. Increasing or decreasing the number of strides will vary the degree of difficulty, and prevent him from anticipating. It will however, deny him the chance of just taking off, and will get him in the frame of mind whereby he is waiting for a command to slow down. Riding this exercise on a circle will add to the steadying effect.

Q.   My horse leans on my hands so much that my arms really ache. He carries his head very low too; is there some way of improving his head carriage so that he is less tiring to ride?

A.   Leaning on the hands can be due to bad conformation,

teeth trouble, being on the forehand (most of the weight sup-
ported over the front legs) or it could be a resistance to the bit
and/or the rider's hands. Conformation cannot be changed. The
mouth should be checked by a vet. Schooling can be worked
on, though, to improve the headcarriage. A horse which is on
its forehand often tends to carry its head rather low, and then
leans on the rider's hands as a means of helping to balance itself.
Use plenty of transitions and some occasional work over poles
on the ground to get him engaging his quarters as much as
possible. As he begins to move his back legs beneath his bodyweight more, so he will support himself on his shoulders and
front legs less, and the headcarriage will become slightly higher.
Take care not to hurry him on too fast, as this will only undo
your schooling work. If he is leaning on your hands out of
resistance, you should try to make your arms as flexible as
possible. If they are stiff and unyielding, he will only set himself
against you. Keep the elbows bent and the wrists slightly
rounded so that you are able to follow the movements of his
head and neck better.

By moving the third fingers slightly on the reins, you can
create a little movement in the bit which will also discourage
him from leaning – although this should never become a sawing
motion, just a barely perceptible movement. A change of bit
might also help. A wire ring bit or one with rollers on the bit
will be less fixed in his mouth and more difficult to evade in
this manner. Check that he is not opening his mouth or crossing
his jaws at the same time; a change of noseband or an adjustment
to the existing one may be needed if he is.

*Q. My pony will not stand still whilst I am trying to mount
him. How can I make him behave – he just walks off without me!*

A.   No horse or pony will stand quietly if it is in any pain or
discomfort, so make sure that his tack fits properly, and is quite
sound. Consider the way in which you are mounting, which
could be prompting this behaviour. Have both of the reins
gathered up in your left hand to give you a firm enough contact
to stop him walking forward, but not so tight that you pull him
backwards. Both reins should be the same length; if one is
shorter than the other he will be pulled off balance, and have
to move around to regain it. He should also be standing
squarely, so that he is able to balance himself against the weight
of a rider mounting from one side. Take a good handful of

mane in the left hand together with the reins. This will help stop you from accidentally pulling on one or both of them, and will give you something firm to pull on should you need it – not something which is likely to move, as the saddle could. When putting your foot in the stirrup, do not dig a toe in his side, but put the foot in the stirrup right up to the instep, so that you can point the toe downwards.

When actually jumping upwards, take hold of the pommel, or the waist of the saddle, rather than the cantle. If you take the back of the saddle, you are likely to pull it over towards yourself, make the horse's back sore, and twist the wooden framework inside the saddle. Spring upwards with plenty of agility; the more slowly you go about it, the more difficult your horse will find it to balance himself. When you land in the saddle, try to land gently, rather than like a ton of lead, and do not suddenly clamp your legs onto his sides. Whenever he moves, scold him, dismount and start again. When he is good, praise him generously. You might find that it will help at first if you can persuade someone to hold him for you. With time, and by sharpening up your mounting technique, he should come to behave himself.

3

Equitation – Jumping

Q. I am entering my horse for some cross country competitions this year, and am working at getting him fit. I am finding though, that even looking after and riding him myself, I am not very fit, getting out of breath very quickly when we are jumping. I don't want to let him down – are there any other things I can do to improve my fitness?

A. Firstly, part of the problem may be due to your holding your breath whilst jumping – it is a common problem to many people, and will invariably leave you short of breath! Talking, singing, or counting to yourself quietly will help to get you breathing more normally. To improve your general level of fitness, you could try jogging, although if you do not find this very enjoyable, there are plenty of other ways; skipping or playing squash are both very good, and also help to develop concentration, co-ordination and the speed of the reflexes, all of which are important when riding cross country. Cycling will also help to get you a bit fitter; you could also go swimming as this will help to increase the lung capacity.

Q. My pony is really bad about being bridled up, so I have been riding him in his headcollar instead. Would it be safe to jump him in a headcollar?

A. It is not safe to ride in a headcollar by itself at any time, let alone try jumping in one. It is more important to look into the cause of his being difficult to bridle up, and deal with that instead. If it is a physical problem, but one which should not stop you from riding, you could use a hackamore temporarily until the problem has cleared up.

Q. My pony won't jump anything over 2', and is also lazy and clumsy when jumping, often knocking fences down. Would athletic jumping help him?

A. Some horses and ponies just are not natural athletes, and a few even seem to have a built in tape measure, so that it is impossible to persuade them to jump higher than the limit they have set for themselves. Age is also another factor to take into consideration; a youngster may be green and unco-ordinated, whilst an old horse may be stiff and unable to perform very athletically any more. Gymnastic exercises are only really beneficial in helping to improve the technique of the animal, it will not enable him to jump any higher, and unless approached with care, would be physically unfair on an older horse, and may upset a younger one not yet ready. For this reason, and also because it means you do not have to keep getting on and off to adjust fences, it is best if such training is done under the supervision of someone experienced in such matters. If your pony is normally lazy, and not just when jumping, you might re-examine your feeding programme. If he is provided with a little more energy, he may well begin to approach all his work with a little more zest and enthusiasm. If he really does lack ability, and does not enjoy jumping as much as you do, you may be better off in the long run to try something else instead, such as dressage or long distance riding.

Q. I should really love to do more jumping, but it absolutely terrifies me. I start to lose my balance, and then I tend to panic!

A. The answer to this is not to attempt to do too much before you are really ready. You need to build your confidence up slowly, taking things in easy stages. Start off with just a single pole on the ground, and walk, trot and canter over this with your stirrups at jumping length. You will soon get used to gauging your distance from it as you approach, and your horse is unlikely to put in a huge and unseating leap over it – just a gentle hop at the most. Lean forward slightly as you pass over the pole, so that you begin to condition yourself to going forward with the horse rather than fighting against it and instinctively leaning backwards. Keep your heels deep, move your seat slightly backwards in the saddle, and push your hands forward slightly, allowing your horse to stretch his neck out, but without losing the rein contact, so that your upper body folds forward over the horse's neck from the hips. This makes for a very secure position, and you will get used to slipping into it at the right moment with practice. Once you are happy with your progress over one pole on the ground, raise to a height of about a foot, and once more trot and canter over it. Hold a handful of mane on the approach if you like, so that you have something to help you keep forward, and to hang onto if you feel you really need it. Do remember to keep looking ahead, and not down at the ground, otherwise you will lose your balance and get left behind. Keep using plenty of leg to maintain the pace – the better your horse is going forward to meet the jump, the more comfortable it will all feel to you. He will probably only hop over this jump, just giving you enough of a feeling that he has left the ground. Only when you feel quite happy about going over it should you make it any larger – do not feel that you have to keep up with your friends. Jumping should be fun for both horse and rider, and you are the best judge as to what height you feel happiest about jumping.

Q. Every time I get to a jump, my pony seems to hesitate, and then jumps it at the last minute, just when I least expect it, which is very unseating. Is there any way of improving her style so that it is more comfortable?

A.   There are several points to consider here; she may be frightened of receiving a jab in the mouth, especially if she is wearing a strong bit such as a pelham or kimblewick. Change to a less damaging, milder bit if required, and try to adopt a better position where you are not hanging onto the reins. If you need to, take hold of a handful of mane or the neckstrap, so that you do not get left behind and inadvertently take a tug on the reins. If you land heavily on her back, then it will also make her uncomfortable and unwilling to jump freely, in case you land even more heavily. If your pony is of an excitable nature, there is also a possibility that you are holding her back so strongly that she is unable to jump fluently. If she is very stiff, she may need to be allowed to move on a bit faster than others in order to clear the jump. If she is a little ploddy, she will need to be pushed on more strongly towards her fences so that she tackles them more positively. You could be partly to blame for this; do not 'freeze' at the last minute, but try and ride on, both before, over, and after, the fence. She will need this help particularly if she is a short striding pony, as this sort do tend to take off and land very close to their fences unless ridden on very vigorously. Do be careful not to overface her either. If you are jumping fences which are rather on the high side for her ability, then an awkward jump is only to be expected, and if you persist she may start refusing.

Q.   My horse has started to refuse at jumps; I have owned him for a year and competed very successfully at shows with him all this summer with no problems whatsoever. Now, all of a sudden, it is a real struggle to get him over even the smallest jump.

A.   This sounds as though your horse has been overjumped. He has evidently done quite a bit of competition work recently, and doubtless has practised at home too. Forget about jumping for the moment, and place the emphasis on letting him enjoy himself; go out for some hacks, and just do a little flatwork to keep him supple and his mind active. The ground can be pretty hard in the summer, and if it has been jarring his legs, then this will also make him understandably reluctant to jump. Once he has had a complete break from jumping, you might find that taking him hunting during the winter will help to restore his enthusiasm for jumping again. When returning to competition work, do be selective, rather than overjumping him – and try not to practise too much at home.

Q.   My horse has got quite a jump – the trouble being that he doesn't always jump clear. Although he is quite capable, he seems to get a bit lazy and will keep brushing against a fence every now and then – even though he could clear it easily if he tried. How can I make him tuck his feet up more?

A.   Athletic jumping often helps to improve jumping technique; teaching the horse to tuck its feet up out of the way, and to use itself correctly over the fence. Unless you are very experienced though, it is best to go to a good instructor for such tuition, as it is easy to do a great deal of damage, and shake the confidence if distances have been wrongly set up. Distances between fences and poles need to be varied slightly according to each animal's length of stride, and what you are trying to achieve, and it does take a good eye and a certain amount of experience to judge what is right. It does sound quite likely in your horse's case though, that his jumping abilities are not so much at fault as his attitude. Don't practise at home, but keep him fresh for shows instead, just popping over the practice fence a couple of times to warm up before the class. That way he will go into the ring taking a good look at everything, and making more of an effort. Too much work over jumps at home will only make him switch off and become rather bored with it all – but you can keep working on his flatwork so that he remains supple and obedient.

Q.   Every time my horse lands after a jump he puts his head right down, shaking it from side to side and putting in little bucks. I have fallen off several times because of this – is there any way of stopping him?

A.   This may be due to either an over-strong or insufficient contact. If it is too strong, then he may well be trying to find some freedom from it on landing, when you are in a less secure position. If it is insufficient, then he may just be taking advantage of the moment to indulge in a little high spirits and naughtiness. Try and develop a more secure position so that you are able to adjust your rein contact to suit you both better. The best way of doing this is to have some lessons at a riding school on a steady horse, and in an enclosed area, so that you can work without your stirrups, and perhaps without your reins too. When jumping your own horse, make sure that you do not give him a chance to idle after jumping a fence. Keep a firm, but steady contact on landing, sit up and ride positively away, rather than waiting for the worst. You might even find that placing a second fence after the first, or having to negotiate a turn will get him concentrating more on the work in hand, and less on larking about. Do not rule out the possibility either that his saddle may be causing him discomfort, or that his back may be twingeing as he uses it over a jump; ask a saddler and a vet to check out these.

Q.   My three-year-old is coming along nicely on the flat, and I would now like to teach her to jump. How do I go about this, or should I wait until she is a bit older?

A.   At three years old, the bones are still very immature, and if overstressed could be permanently damaged. Leave jumping until she is four, when you can begin to introduce her first to a single pole on the ground, and then to lines of three poles at equal distances from each other. The distance apart may vary from about 4'3"–5' according to her natural length of stride and height. If she has to fit in the occasional hop or half stride, they are too far apart, whilst if the stride becomes stilted, they are too close together. When the distance is correct, there should be no difference in the stride, other than an increased degree of elevation and activity, and a lowering of the head and neck. When she is working calmly over these in trot, introduce a small crosspole fence with a single pole just in front of it. This will need to be positioned approximately 9' away from the fence. Using a cross pole as the obstacle will help to get her into the habit of jumping straight, and at the centre of the fence. It should be kept fairly low to start with – about 18″ at the centre will be quite sufficient. Once quite confident and quietly trotting over this sort of jump, you can progress to small uprights of about 2′–2′6″. Rather than increase the height, try to change the type of jump, so that she becomes used to variety, and learns to take it all in her stride. You could begin to do a little jumping out of canter too, (remove the pole on the approach) and when you feel she is ready, introduce some small parallels. Even at this age, she will be more susceptible to injury than a more mature horse, and you should try and avoid doing too much, especially when the ground is hard. Jumping practice can be restricted to perhaps twice a week – you do not want her to become bored by it either. Once she is five, you can begin to concentrate more seriously on her jumping if she shows talent in that direction, and give her some experience in small jumping classes. But it is worth taking it steadily whilst she is still young.

Q. I keep falling off when I am jumping, usually just as my horse is landing. He seems almost to slow down, and his head seems very low, so that I lose my balance. I am covered in bruises, and getting very disheartened. How can I stay on top?

A. Two things need to be done; your position must be improved, and you must ride on more energetically as you are landing. Keep your heels deep, and watch that your lower leg does not slip backwards, which will otherwise make your position weak and unbalanced. Sit up more quickly as you land, and you should then find it easier to both stay on board and rebalance him so that his head does not seem so low. You will also find it easier to use your legs, which will correct his head carriage a little; it will also make him move away from the fence quicker on landing, so that you do not end up with him stopping, and you continuing on your own.

Q. My horse tries to rush off each time we land after a fence, so that it is really difficult to turn in time for the next jump when I am in a competition. How can I slow him down a bit?

A. Do be careful that you do not land in the saddle with a crash each time you land, otherwise your horse may try to run away from the anticipated pain. He sounds the enthusiastic type who is keen to get on with the job in hand. This means that you will need to speed up your own reactions if you are to remain in control. If your reins are in loops as he lands, he is bound to get away from you, so keep a firm contact throughout all phases of the jump. You must know the course thoroughly, and be ready to give him instructions about where he is going next, otherwise he will take things into his own hands. When schooling at home, you could try jumping him through doubles, or placing a pole between 21'–24' away on the landing side, to encourage him to steady a little and think about where he is going.

Q. My horse often takes off too far away from the jump, which takes me by surprise. When jumping spreads, it also means that he often knocks the back pole down; is there any method of getting him to take off closer?

A. When schooling, avoid 'staircase' or ascending spreads. Use either upright fences, or true parallels, with the front and back poles at the same height. Make sure that there is some kind of groundline, and that it is not pulled forward (towards the horse) in front of the jump. Do not approach too fast, but keep a steady pace, and look towards either the centre or bottom of the fence, not out over the top of it. If you have the occasional jumping lesson, ask your instructor to show you the right distance at which to place a pole on the ground in front of the jump to encourage him to take off closer to it. Working over jumps in trot will also encourage him to get closer before taking off.

Q. My pony jumps very crookedly, so that when we are jumping doubles or trebles, he goes so far across to the left that he either runs out, or bumps my foot on the wings. How can I straighten this out?

A. School at home over some cross poles – this will keep him more central, and make him tuck his feet up beneath himself rather than twisting them to one side. You could also put up a diagonal pole from the left side of the fence to try and keep him approaching the middle. Carry your stick in your left hand, and when you feel him beginning to swing across in that direction, give him a sharp smack on that shoulder. Be ready to use your seat and legs more on each approach to keep him straight. If he jumps crookedly, it will not only prove injurious to one

Fig. 10. A suitable fence to help correct a horse which jumps crookedly across to the left.

or other of you, but means that he is less likely to be able to clear a wide spread, and will make the distance between combinations longer than it should be.

4

Saddlery and Horse Clothing

Q. When I am riding, I can hear a strange creaking noise. I can't hear it at any other time – is this a problem with my horse or my saddlery?

A. It sounds as though you should check the saddle over. New saddles do sometimes squeak a lot, so give it a good application of neatsfoot, or some proprietary brand of saddle oil. If however, this saddle is not new, then the noise could be due to a broken tree inside it; this is constructed of beechwood reinforced at points with steel, and is very prone to damage if the saddle is dropped or otherwise mishandled. A broken tree is eventually going to damage your horse's back, so take it to a saddler to be checked over.

Q. My saddle recently got soaked in a rainstorm. I oiled and then soaped it, but the surface seems to have become furry and spongy on the seat. As it is an expensive saddle and I have tried to look after it, I'd like to try and sort it out. Is there a special preparation I can use?

A. The condition described usually only occurs if the leather has become oversaturated with water, and the fibres begin to separate. Whenever leather gets soaked it should be washed to remove any dirt and then allowed to dry naturally in a cool, rather than warm, place. Once it is completely dry it can then be oiled thoroughly to restore any grease it has lost. This should not be done whilst it is still damp, otherwise the oil will not penetrate (oil and water do not mix, and the oil would just sit in a film on the surface and do no good at all). The best thing that you can do with your saddle is to ignore it for a while. Rather than using further preparations, just give it a wipe over with a damp cloth after use, but stop oiling it at all, and let it dry out until the seat is hard and shiny, when you can treat it as normal again.

Q. I recently purchased a new black saddle, since when I've discovered that the dye keeps coming out of it – the seat of my jodhpurs becomes black every time I ride. I've tried washing the leather thoroughly, but it doen't seem to make any difference. The saddler I bought it from won't change it, and said to keep washing it – what should I do? I can't afford to buy another saddle, and I am quite happy with this one in other respects.

A. Follow the advice you have already been given. It is not the fault of the saddler, but rather of whoever processed the leather initially. The dye will normally tend to come out of any leather which has been coloured, unless it has been given a plasticised surface, and black dye is particularly unstable. Even when buying new saddlery which has not been coloured, still give it a thorough wash before use, as water-based dyes are also used along raw edges where the leather has been cut. Otherwise the dye will be washed out upon the hair if the horse becomes sweaty or the leather wet – which could be disastrous in a showing class. Continue to wash the saddle after each use, using fairly hot water with a little washing up liquid added to it, so that you remove as much of the dye as possible; oil and soap it afterwards each time so that the leather does not dry out, but begins to take on its own natural colour.

Q. My four year old mare is difficult to get a bridle on; she just won't open her mouth to take the bit. When she does she then puts her head right up in the air so that I can't reach to put the headpiece over her ears. Is there any way of making her more co-operative?

A. Ask your vet to rule out any possibility of physical problems, which might include sharp teeth, ulcers, lampas, or an ear infection; or at her age she may well be teething and feeling some discomfort because of it. Make sure that the bridle and bit are also comfortable, since all these factors will contribute to awkwardness. If there are no physical problems, ensure that you are completely blameless for her behaviour – avoid banging her teeth with the bit when putting the bridle on or taking it off, as this will make her less than co-operative. You might also try holding a few pieces of carrot, or horse and pony cubes together with the bit on the palm of your hand to encourage her to open her mouth and consider it all as being a pleasant experience. If she does not improve after making these allowances, she is simply being a little naughty, and you should try to place yourself in a position which gives you greater control whilst bridling up. Stand beside your mare, holding the bit on

Fig. 11. Putting on a bridle.

the palm of your left hand. Encircle her nose with your right arm, holding the cheekpieces of the bridle in your right hand. If she tries to raise her head you will then be able to prevent her by pressing down on her nose with your right hand. Offer the bit on the palm of your left hand; if she won't open her mouth slide your thumb in at the corner where there are no teeth, and press it down on her tongue. As she opens her mouth, quickly slip the bit in and raise the cheekpieces upwards with your right hand so that it does not slip out again. Then use your left hand to push her ears through the headpiece. If you are fairly short, try standing on an upturned bucket or box (but something fairly stable) so that you have the advantage of height as well.

Q.   My pony's New Zealand rug seems to be letting in an awful lot of water – the rain seems to go right through it, and it was new last winter. Is there anything I can do to make it more waterproof?

A.   If you cleaned the rug with detergent last Spring before storing it, it will need reproofing to completely waterproof it again. You can buy tins of reproofing wax from most saddlers. Some rugs do let a lot of water in through the seams, even though they are well waterproofed elsewhere, but you can deal with this problem most effectively by rubbing candlewax along them to seal them.

Q.   The legstraps on my horse's New Zealand rug seem to rub him a lot – he gets very sore around his back legs and a lot of the hair has been rubbed away. Would it be better to cut the straps off completely?

A.   If you do this, the rug is very likely to slip if he rolls, which could be more dangerous than leaving the straps on; the back may also flap forwards if it is windy, leaving him with little protection from the cold and wet, and possibly frightening him into the bargain. Make sure that you are not fastening them too tightly, and if they are made of leather, keep them clean and well oiled so that they are soft, supple and less likely to chafe. Nylon straps should also be kept as clean as possible. Check the rug at least twice each day – if it has slipped straighten it, otherwise this will eventually cause soreness around the shoulders as well as around the legs. The legstraps can be lined, by slipping a length of bicycle tyre inner tubing over them. Your saddler could also make some slots in the sides of the rug to thread the surcingle through (if one is used) and add darts to the back for a better fit, less likely to slip: alternatively use crossing belly straps and a fillet string to replace the leg straps altogether.

Q.   My gelding's rugs slip a lot in the stable, and I often find him shivering with cold the next morning. He is clipped and I worry that he will get chilled, but am at a loss as to how to keep everything in place.

A.   There are several things which can be done. If the rugs always slip to one side, say to the left, then fasten the roller on the right hand side, and position the rugs so that they lie slightly more to the right hand side too. If this does not work, then ask your saddler to attach some legstraps, as on a New Zealand rug, which may solve the problem, especially if the legstrap on the opposite side to which the rug tends to slip is fastened a little shorter. Another alternative is to get your sad-dler to attach some crossing belly straps on the rug which you can use instead of, or as well as, a roller. These do seem to be very successful in keeping rugs in place.

You should also check of course, that the rugs you are using are not causing discomfort because they do not fit properly. Some horses are allergic to certain fibres, which makes them more inclined to try and dislodge them. If the rug is tailored as much as possible to the shape of the animal, so much the better, and it often helps if you ask your saddler to put darts

Fig. 12. Crossing belly straps and darts.

or a drawstring over the quarters of it. Two breast straps, rather than a single one also seem to help.

Q. I've got a numnah made out of real sheepskin, but it is getting rather dirty. How should I go about cleaning it?

A. If it isn't too grubby, you could sprinkle a little talcum powder on it and then brush it out, as this will absorb some of the sweat and dirt. Look at the label on it too, as some of these numnahs are washable. If so, use a soft soap and warm water, rinsing thoroughly. Allow it to dry naturally, kneading it occasionally to prevent it from becoming stiff. If it is not washable, then you will have to get it dry cleaned.

Q. My horse lives out all the year round and so has developed a very oily coat to protect himself from the weather. My tack gets very greasy because of this, and it is terrible trying to keep everything clean. Are there any quick ways of getting the grease off? Also, when I have soaped it, the leather always seems to look dull, and never has a nice sheen on it – could I be doing something wrong?

A. Use a thin quilted cotton numnah, which will help to protect the saddle lining without actually altering the fit of the saddle. This will be easy to keep clean, as all you need to do is pop it in the washing machine when it gets dirty. When you wash your tack, use a few drops of washing up liquid in the water, which also needs to be fairly hot if you are to get rid of all the grease. This will make your job a lot easier; any really stubborn 'jockeys' of grease can be removed by gently teasing them off with a fingernail. Try and clean your tack fairly frequently – even if you only have time to give it a quick wipe over each time it is used, it will still save you from having a mammoth task on your hands at the end of each week. It is important to keep your tack as clean as possible, not just from the point of view of safety and prolonging its life, but also to keep your pony free from sores and galls.

Q. I have always tried to take good care of my saddle, cleaning it every time it is used. I now find however, that it feels very greasy and unpleasant – how can I correct this?

A.   It sounds very much as though the leather has been over-nourished. Wash it thoroughly with very hot, regularly changed, water which has had a few drops of washing up liquid added to it. Wash it less often, and use rather less soap, instead of overdoing it: after riding, a wipe over with a damp cloth will be sufficient on most occasions, with more thorough attention once a week.

Q. Every time I put a tail bandage on my horse it never seems to stay put, no matter how tightly I try and put it on, or even if someone else does it. I am not sure, since I have never caught him at it, but I think he must be rubbing it off, as his tail is always a mess afterwards. Is there any way I can keep it in place?

A.   The most effective way is to buy a tail guard and put this over the tail bandage. You will need to put a roller on as well

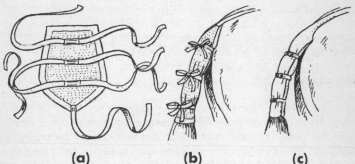

(a)   (b)   (c)

Fig. 13.
(a) A tail guard made from rugging.
(b) A rugging tail guard on a horse.
(c) A leather tail guard on a horse.
The long tape at the top of the tail attaches to the roller or surcingle.

to which you can attach the topmost tapes, to prevent it from sliding downwards. One made of rugging is not too expensive (or you could easily make your own) but if you find that your horse is really determined to get it off, you might have to splash out and buy a leather tail guard which will not tear. Do make sure that there is not some cause for this irritation; wash his tail regularly so that it is less itchy, but make sure that all the soap is washed out completely or it will be scurfy and he will rub at it anyway. Check also for signs of worm infestation, or the onset of some skin disorder, which could cause him to rub his tail vigorously.

Q.   We have had a lot of saddlery thefts in our area, some from even quite well locked tackrooms. Are there any ways in which I can protect my saddlery, since although it is insured, it would still be very inconvenient if it was stolen?

A.   You should of course make sure that any rooms used for storage of saddlery are locked and padlocked, and windows are barred or bolted in some manner to make access more difficult. A burglar alarm should also be fitted, and you could also security mark your tack. If you contact your local police station, they are prepared (at no cost) to mark your tack with your name, postcode, or whatever you wish, using a metal stamp to indent the leather. These should be re-done occasionally as they do tend to grow fainter, but can prove to be a means of tracing, and recovering, stolen items. It is effective as a deterrent too, since a label can be stuck up on the wall inside the room, in a prominent position, stating that everything is security marked. Notices to this effect should not, however, be posted outside, nor any other signs which advertise the fact that saddlery is stored there.

Q.   I'd like to clip my horse, but have a problem in that he tears his rugs. I can't clip him without rugging him up as he does feel the cold, but the rugs I put on him are in tatters within minutes. He is desperately in need of clipping as he is getting so hot when I ride – but I can hardly go ahead if I can't keep him warm.

A.   There is really only one solution with a horse which tears its rugs, and that is to put a muzzle or a clothing bib on him. Either of these can be bought from your saddler, but you should make sure that the headcollar you use fits well and won't rub.

Although it is possible to use a bucket-type muzzle without a headcollar, it does make sense to attach it to one, or else it can

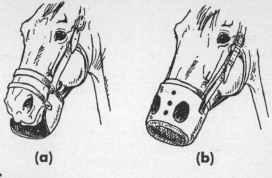

(a) (b)

Fig. 14.
(a) Bib muzzle.
(b) Bucket muzzle.

be easily dislodged over one ear. Look for any obvious reasons for this habit too – ensure that his rugs are not irritating him in any way. If you are overrugging him in your anxiety to keep him warm for example, he may be getting too hot, and will look for ways of removing his clothing. Similarly, if he is uncomfortable because the rugs are a bad fit, or the roller/surcingle is too tight, or pinching, he will also look for ways to escape the discomfort.

Q. How should I go about washing my rugs ready to put away for next year? And how should they be stored?

A. Brush all the linings first of all to remove the worst of the stable stains and any loose hairs. Jute rugs can be spread out on the yard, and scrubbed by hand with water and washing powder. Alternatively, you may prefer to do them in the bath, or even in the washing machine, if it is large and sturdy enough. Most synthetic rugs are washable, many by machine, and are less bulky on the whole, but the individual manufacturers' instructions should be followed in such cases. New Zealand rugs can be scrubbed in the same way as jute rugs, but detergents should not be used as they are rather harsh, and will remove the proofing. Scrubbing will remove some of the proofing anyway, and so once they are dry they should be reproofed again with wax available at the saddlers. Any necessary repairs should be made before storing, which can be done by placing them in large polythene bags with a few mothballs. These can then be labelled so that the contents are identifiable again, and they can be placed somewhere dry, such as a loft.

Q. I have just sold my pony, but probably won't get another one for at least a year. I would like to hang onto the saddle and bridle though, but am not sure how to go about storing them.

A. Wash the leather first of all, taking everything apart. Then soap it, followed by Kao-cho-line (available from a saddler) which will help to prevent it from drying out or becoming mouldy. Wrap a sheet around everything to keep the dust out and store somewhere dry, preferably away from direct heat or sunlight. If possible store the saddle on a wooden horse to avoid damage, or else upright, on the pommel.

Q. How often should I get my saddle reflocked?

A. The flocking, or stuffing, inside the panels of the saddle, is usually fairly soft in new saddles. It packs down quite quickly and will need further attention sometime during the first year. After that, it should be checked thoroughly every six months, or at any time when the saddle does not fit the horse, or tips the rider forwards or backwards. Remember that horses and ponies can change shape quite dramatically according to the amount and type of exercise (or lack of it) they receive and so this must be taken into account. Sometimes it may be necessary to remove flock, rather than increase it – if the animal has suddenly put on a lot of weight, for example. Occasionally it may be found that the flock has become lumpy, which can cause pressure points on the horse's back, and tender areas as a result, and in such cases, all the flock is removed and replaced.

Q. I am going to buy a horse shortly – what are the basics that I can expect to buy for it?

A. Your requirements will vary according to whether you intend to keep your horse stabled, or living out. You should be able to manage with far less if he lives out for example. Start off with the essentials, so that you will at least have everything necessary to hand initially, and then later on you can add to them as you wish. If he is to be living out he will need:
Bridle (plus bit and martingale if required)
General Purpose saddle, buckle guards, stirrup leathers and irons

Girth
Headcollar and lead rope
New Zealand rug
Grooming kit
Tack cleaning equipment
First Aid kit
Fly fringe and/or repellent
plus numnah if desired.
If he is to be stabled, either all or part of the time, he will need, in addition:
Jute or stable rug
Roller/Surcingle
Sweat sheet
Mucking out tools (wheelbarrow, pitchfork, shovel, broom, and skep)

Q.   I cannot afford to buy a new saddle, and wonder what problems, if any, are attached to buying secondhand tack?

A.   This is a difficulty which many people have to face, but often it can be better in the long run to save up the extra and buy new saddlery if at all possible. Ask a reputable saddler to come and fit the tack to your horse which saves a lot of running back and forth, and allows you to try a range of different saddles or rugs in order to find the best fit. It gives you the benefit of an informed and experienced opinion.

It can often be difficult for the inexperienced person to pick out a genuine bargain from the 'rubbish' when buying second-hand. So, if this is the only recourse open to you, you should certainly avoid auctions, and ask an informed person to come along and help advise you. Apart from the obvious problems, such as that the equipment must suit both horse and rider, there can be many other hidden pitfalls. Don't rush into anything if you are not entirely satisfied with it. If major repairwork looks to be necessary, buying secondhand can prove to be anything but economical.

Check the state of the leather – it should be firm and greasy, with no signs of wrinkling or blistering. Look carefully at points where leather has been in contact with metal ie the bit, stirrup irons, buckles, as these may prove to be worn and weakened. If the flaps, seat, or panels of a saddle are very worn, you should take this into account when negotiating a price, as repairing these areas will be costly, and may even look unsightly. Tug gently at any stitching to see if it is safe; re-stitching in most areas does not cost much, but in certain areas such as around the saddleflaps, it is likely to require frequent maintenance. Bridlework which has been backstitched (this looks like one continuous stitch on the reverse side) is usually indicative of poor quality workmanship and cheap materials, and is also very likely to rub. Metal fittings, including buckles and hook studs, should be of good quality, in good condition, not worn with age.

Indian saddlery should be avoided; the workmanship nowadays, and design, are far better than they were a few years ago, but the materials used still tend to be of inferior quality, and often unsafe. Indian leather can be identified by an unpleasant pungent smell if it is still reasonably new, combined with a distinctive yellowish colouring. It is less pleasant to the touch, may sometimes be heavily grained, and the saddles are often flocked up with something resembling multicoloured carpet-waste.

Check the girth straps, and the webbs that they are attached to; there should be three on each side of the saddle, and in good condition. Replacement is fairly easy if necessary, and may be worthwhile if the saddle is otherwise in good condition, but a reduction in price could be sought on account of the expense. A broken tree (the beechwood framework inside the

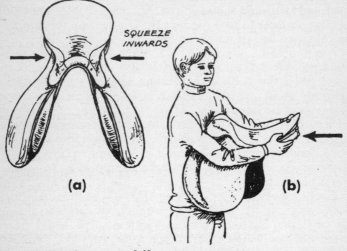

Fig. 15. Testing a saddle tree across:
(a) the front arch, and
(b) the waist.

saddle) is probably one of the more serious hazards to avoid, and can be detected by an excessive amount of movement, and possibly squeaking too, when it is tested by pressing the 'points' towards each other, or the cantle and pommel towards each other. This is a test though, which really needs to be performed by somebody who knows what to look for, as 'spring' trees are more flexible than 'rigid' ones and can be deceptive.*

Q. I have just bought a few secondhand rugs – are there any precautions I should take before using them?

A. Before using any secondhand saddlery or horse clothing, you should disinfect it thoroughly first to try and ensure that any skin diseases the last occupant may have had are not passed on. You can do this by using a fairly strong solution of Milton Sterilising Fluid, which can be bought from most chemists, and is unlikely to irritate the skin. You should also do the same if your tack has ever gone mouldy, as ordinary washing will not kill the spores, which can set up a nasty irritation.

Q. My mare is very bad about having her saddle put on – she hunches her back up and snaps whilst I am trying to do the girth up – how can I stop her from doing this?

A. It would be wise to rule out the possibility of any physical discomfort first by getting the vet to check her back, and your saddler to inspect the fit of the saddle. When putting the saddle on, do be careful to place it gently on her back, slightly further forward than necessary, and then to slide it back into position so that all the hairs lie flat and in the right direction beneath. She may well be rather sensitive to the initial contact of the saddle too, and you may find it helps to use a numnah between the saddle and her back. You should pull the front of it well up into the front arch of the saddle so that it doesn't press onto the withers. When tightening the girth, do it firmly but not abruptly, and not overtightly. Both of the buckles on each side of the girth should lie level with each other to eliminate the danger of pinching as much as possible. To this same end, each of the front legs should be picked up and stretched forwards,

---

*A more detailed explanation regarding the fitting and purchase of saddlery and equipment, both new and secondhand, can be found by referring to 'Buying and Fitting Saddlery' by the same authors in the 'Paperfront' series.

so that any loose skin or hair is not caught up beneath. After this, walk her around in hand for five minutes or so, to give the saddle time to settle down on her back before tightening the girth completely and mounting. With a tactful approach, you should find that she will gradually become more amenable.

Q. Every winter, my pony gets rub marks around his withers, on his back where the surcingle goes over his spine, and down the sides of his shoulders. Apart from the fact that this must be rather uncomfortable for him, it takes a long time for the hair to grow out again, so that he always looks awful with bald patches on him! Is there any way of preventing this from happening?

A. Make sure that your rugs fit properly; if they are tight around the shoulders they will rub him as he moves around, whilst if they are prone to slip, they will rub as they slide round. You could also pad the shoulders with pieces of real or synthetic sheepskin, and stitch two pieces of foam on either side of the withers. This will not only help to keep the rugs from slipping, but will lift the rug off the withers, and so preventing rubbing in this area. When stabled, use a thick piece of foam rubber beneath the surcingle or roller, to prevent excessive pressure on the spine, which will make him sore. When he is out in the field in his New Zealand rug, stitch a piece of foam into the lining on either side of his spine, which will do the same job, but without the foam becoming lost or muddy. Stitch the surcingle into place on the rug too, leaving a slack loop in it where it passes over the spine – or alternatively, substitute crossing belly straps and a fillet string.

Q. There is a movable catch on the end of the stirrup bar on my saddle; should this be left up or down?

A. The catch (known as the 'thumbpiece') should always be left down. It is a safety precaution, since should your foot become trapped in a stirrup iron, you will only be dragged a short distance before the leather slips off the stirrup bar, so freeing you. The only time the thumbpiece should be turned upwards is when you are taking the saddle somewhere, i.e. to a show, or the saddlers, in which case it will stop you from inadvertently losing a leather and iron.

5

Grazing and Fencing

Q. I have started looking around for some suitable grazing in preparation for the pony I shall shortly be buying. How big a field should I look for? And what sort of qualities should it have?

A. It is not always possible to pick and choose your grazing as much as you would like. Even when you can, it is still far from easy to find somewhere which could be classed as 'perfect'! It should, however, be large enough to support the number of animals expected to graze it, otherwise the land will quickly become sour and worm-infested so that it is left not only useless but harmful. You should be able to keep one pony on one acre of land (provided it is regularly rested and properly maintained). Larger areas tend to suffer less from selective grazing and poaching of ground, and can normally support about 1000 – 1400 lbs of animal weight per acre if it is in good condition. When choosing a paddock, look at the state of the fencing – it should all be in good repair if accidents are not to happen. Check that there is a good regular supply of fresh water. If you have to refill containers continually you will soon become disenchanted, whilst ponds are less than ideal since they often become stagnant.

Adequate shelter should be available; even if your horse or pony is to be kept partially stabled; there will be occasions when he will be glad of it. Such shelter could be provided by a building, or by natural features such as a hedge or line of trees. The grass itself should be neither overlush, such as the type used for raising cattle, nor should it be so poor as to be totally lacking in nutritional value. Good pasture consists of at least 25% perennial ryegrass, mixed with cocksfoot, timothy, meadow fescue, sheeps fescue, and bent grasses, together with useful herbs such as yarrow, clover, burnet, chicory, and dandelion forming about a tenth. Avoid pasture which has poisonous plants growing in it, since many of these are a sign of poor quality grazing, and all are dangerous and will need removing before a pony can safely be allowed to graze. You may feel

51

more wary renting or buying grazing in certain areas. Near towns, and where footpaths cross the field, there may be the danger of animals being teased, or even maliciously let out. Security is important in such cases, and it is worth freezemarking all the animals, and putting a stout padlock and chain on both sides of the gate so that it can neither be opened nor lifted off its hinges. The field itself and the perimeters should also be regularly checked in case rubbish has been thoughtlessly thrown in, or fencing damaged.

Q. What sort of plants are dangerous to my pony? And how should I get rid of such poisonous plants?

A.　Poisonous plants can be a real problem, and you should keep a careful eye out for them when making a daily check of the field; even if your field is apparently clear when you first rent it, seeds can still be carried by the wind, and plants start to grow later. Such plants to avoid include acorns, green oak leaves, yew, privet, ragwort, cowbane, Deadly Nightshade, Water Dropwort, Aconite, Bracken, Horsetail, Meadow Saffron, and ivy. Some species of buttercup are also toxic, and although not fatal can cause some unpleasant symptoms including paralysis of the salivary glands. Some of these plants may also be more palatable dead than alive, and so should always be removed from the field and burnt if they have been pulled or sprayed, or the animals removed until the plants are completely desiccated.

Hay should always be shaken out before feeding, as it can sometimes contain poisonous plants if it comes from poor quality pasture, which if not noticed, may be ingested with fatal results. Pulling by hand is easiest when the ground is slightly wet, but often fails to remove the roots completely, and is in any case time-consuming. It is far more effective to spray with a weedkiller; the Ministry of Agriculture locally can advise the most suitable product to use, and provide a fuller list of poisonous plants.

Q. There are a lot of weeds in my field, which rather seem to be taking it over and stifling the grass. What is the best way of removing them?

A.　Weeds are commonly a sign of badly drained or infertile soil, and the best way of eradicating them is to deal with these two problems, as well as spraying. If drainage is bad (sometimes

PERENNIAL
RYEGRASS

TIMOTHY

COCKSFOOT

MEADOW
FESCUE

SHEEPS
FESCUE

BENT
GRASS

YARROW

CLOVER

BURNET

CHICORY

DANDELION

Fig. 16. Types of grasses and herbs.

OAK   YEW   PRIVET   RAGWORT

COWBANE   DEADLY   WATER   ACONITE
             NIGHTSHADE   DROPWORT

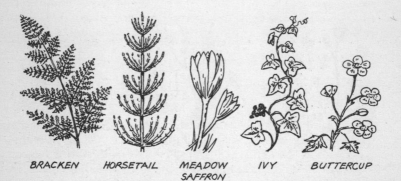

BRACKEN   HORSETAIL   MEADOW   IVY   BUTTERCUP
                        SAFFRON

Fig. 17. Poisonous plants.

it is so bad that pools of water can be seen sitting on the surface)
the air pockets in the soil become filled with moisture, and the
grass roots are starved of oxygen and thus do not develop. This
sort of soil is also cold. You may need to seek expert advice
and have a survey done properly so that a system with correct
spacing and infill material is set up which is suitable for the
type of soil. Check first for yourself that the problem does not
lie in blocked up existing drainage ditches and outlets. If you
need further advice, you could consult a local agricultural contractor.

Before fertilising a field, you should first have a soil analysis
performed; this needs to be done every 4 – 5 years. This will
be provided on request by the Ministry of Agriculture, and they
will be able to tell you what is required. It is no good just adding
things willy-nilly or you could upset the balance of nutrients
already present. It is worth a little effort to improve your pasture; remember that the quality of grass is only going to be as
good as the soil beneath it, and good grass can provide a large
proportion of your horse or pony's diet.

*Q. My field is in such a terrible state that I am wondering
whether it is worth ploughing it up and re-seeding it?*

A. Such a task is very much a last resort, and not really one
to be undertaken by the amateur; you will need assistance from
a local farmer or agricultural contractor. You will also be unable
to use the land for horses to graze for several months, and it
will be unsuitable in any case for some time for youngsters.
You should find though, that correct grazing management, fertilising and harrowing can improve a pasture considerably over
just a few years.

Q. What sort of maintenance does my field require?

A. If you do not actually own the grazing but lease it, first
check to find out who is responsible for any maintenance, and
to what degree. However good your intentions may be, you
cannot simply trample on the toes of the owner of the land –
or at least not without asking permission first! As far as maintenance is concerned, a soil analysis should be performed every
4 – 5 years, and fertilisers then added as required. Small areas
especially need careful management, and will need to be rested
occasionally. Larger areas of land often benefit from being
divided into smaller ones which can be grazed in rotation, so

giving the grass a chance to recover. The horses should be moved on when the grass is short – but not bare. Bare grazing will burn up easily in the summer heat, encourage weeds, and take a long time to recover.

Reintroduce the horses to the grazing again when the grass is about 4"–5" long. If it is longer it begins to lose its nutritional value, and there will be waste as a lot will be trampled down. Cattle grazing in rotation with horses is beneficial, if the former are allowed to follow through afterwards. They are less selective grazers, and will eat coarser grass left by horses and help to break the worm cycle, since they are not natural hosts of the same parasites. If grazing with cattle is not practical, the ranker patches of grass can be mown to allow room for younger, sweeter shoots to grow without being stifled. In small areas, you can pick up the droppings on a daily basis. If left longer than this, the surrounding grass will become sour and the area ignored.

It is also worth harrowing your grazing each Spring in late February/March, as it will remove moss and dead grass left

Fig. 18. Harrowing.

after the winter. If fertilising afterwards, it also helps to open the ground up a bit more, making it quicker and easier for the fertiliser to absorbed. Either a farmer or agricultural contracttor will be able to do this job; the only implement which will be of any use is a heavy spiked or pitchpole type harrow. Dragging a branch across the field behind a car does no good whatsoever – in fact if anything it is more likely to damage the soil structure.

Q. If my horse is grazing a large field, is it still necessary to worm him as often as if he was on a small field?

A.   Regular worming is very important. Although it is impossible to get rid of them completely they must be controlled if the animal is to remain in good health. For this reason, paddocks must be properly managed, and all the animals wormed – regardless of the size of the field – every six to eight weeks. They should also be wormed all at the same time if it is to be effective, otherwise one will continually be ingesting the eggs from the others. Change the wormer used once a year, as a degree of immunity can be built up. Do not just change the product name, but look to see what the anthelmintic contained is, and change that.

Q.   *What is the best type of fencing to have?*

A.   If they are in good order, hedges or stone walls make excellent fencing for horses, since they also provide plenty of shelter. Hedges however, need to be very thick, strong, and well maintained if they are to keep the animals in, and since they can often harbour poisonous plants, it is sometimes best to build another inner fence, whilst leaving the hedge to provide some shelter. Stone walls are found in certain upland areas, but again should be regularly checked as to the state of repair, and any fallen stones picked up and replaced. Post and rail fencing looks very smart and is perhaps the ideal fencing, but is very expensive, requiring a minimum of three rails to make an imposing fence. Most people have to settle for the cheaper option of using wire; this should be the plain, heavy gauge type, and needs to be maintained with care. Strong, solidly erected straining posts are needed, and the wires must be kept taut and any missing staples fastening the wire to the wood should be replaced immediately. A straining eyebolt or a ratchet-type strainer should be used for each wire at an end post. Ideally, a top wooden rail should be put up to form an easily seen barrier (or strips of coloured plastic can be tied onto the wires) and the lowest strand of wire should be at least one foot from the ground so that the feet do not become caught up.

Barbed wire is not a good fencing at all, as some horrific accidents can result from horses becoming caught up; it also tends to pull the mane out when they reach underneath it. If you have no other choice (for example if you have to share your grazing with cattle) then you will simply have to ensure that the strands are always kept taut, and a pair of wire cutters should be kept nearby in case of an emergency. Electric fencing is not reliable as a form of permanent fencing, but it can be a

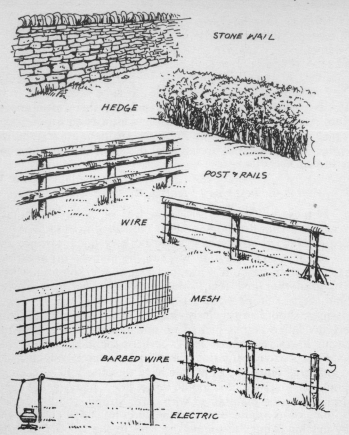

Fig. 19. Types of fencing.

useful way of dividing grazing in order either to rest it, or to allow it to grow for hay. It is easy to set up, and to move around as required. It needs checking at least twice a day to ensure that the current running through the wire is not being earthed by tall weeds or anything else. Horses or ponies unused to electric fencing shoud be led up to it and around the boundary before allowing them loose, so that they have some respect for it, and idea of the location. Strips of coloured plastic hung on the wire, or one of the types of electric fencing designed with horses in mind will be more clearly visible.

Meshed wire fencing is also popular these days, and provided the mesh is fine enough, will prevent legs from being pushed through the fence, or grazing beneath bottom rails or wires.

Q. My paddock is very small, and I would like to tether my horse on the local common as a means of providing some extra grazing.

A.   Tethering may sound like the ideal solution if your grazing is limited, or if you cannot find any proper pasture, but in reality it is almost as much hassle as keeping the animal stabled, and can be quite dangerous. You will need to provide some source of water, whilst the grass may be very inferior, and is quite likely to contain rubbish and poisonous plants. Once he has eaten the grass in his immediate area he will then need to be moved again. Lack of shelter can make life miserable, whilst passers-by and children stopping to feed tit-bits can turn even

Fig. 20. A tethered pony.

the most placid pony into a tyrant. Besides this, if he is unused to being tethered, there is a danger that he will get tangled up, panic and badly injure himself. You will need to keep an eye on him all the time at first to make sure that he learns how to cope with his chain. It would altogether be far kinder, as well as more practical, to search around a bit harder and find some properly fenced land.

Q. My pony is really bad about being caught, which is very tiresome when I particularly want to get somewhere for a certain time.

A.   This is a habit which will take some time to cure; you may be able to catch him on occasion by cornering him – but this obviously requires quite a few people, is impractical when you are on your own, and will not make him any easier to catch. If you are to eventually be able to catch him unaided whenever you want to, then he must come to associate it with something pleasant. This means that a long term view needs to be taken, and although at first there may be days when you cannot get near him, there will be others when he is fine, and these will increase.

Try to catch him at least once a day; when you are successful, bring him in and give him a small feed. Do not catch him just to ride him, or he will continue to be wary. Make a fuss of him, give him a quick brush over and check his feet, and then turn him out again. He will begin to look forward to your visits when he knows that there will be a treat for him, and it does not always involve working. Leave a snugly fitting headcollar on him with a short length of rope attached to it, as this will make it easier for you to catch him. When the grass improves in the summer, you may find that he reverts to his old ways, and if it is impossible to catch him on your own, may have to consider using hobbles, or moving him to a barer piece of grazing and supplying him with extra supplementary feed instead.

Q.   My pony keeps jumping out of his field, and I am worried that he will either injure himself one day doing so, or be hurt whilst he is out. How can I keep him in?

A.   Unless he is on a diet, first make sure that he is not hungry and simply going in search of more food. Some horses and ponies do seem to enjoy the challenge of escaping from their surroundings though, in which case you will have to either make the fence so high that he is unable to jump it, or to hobble him. If he lives on his own, advertising to share your grazing with, or buying him a companion might encourage him to stay put.

6

Stabling, Bedding, and Stable Equipment

Q. How can I stop my pony from kicking over his water bucket? He keeps doing it, and so is always very thirsty the next morning when he has no water left.

A. This can be a really annoying habit, as well as an expensive one, since the bedding inevitably becomes soaked through and has to be thrown out. There are several solutions. You could, for example, install an automatic watering system, although this will need to be well lagged to prevent it from freezing up in the winter months. They are quite expensive, however, and if he starts to play with the water, can end up leaving the bed just as wet. You could alternatively, place his water bucket in the centre of a tyre, or else buy a plastic dustbin to use as a water container. These are easy to clean out, (and must be emptied daily otherwise the water becomes stale) and once filled are so heavy that they cannot be knocked over.

Q. My horse has started nipping people over the stable door – I think that a lot of this is due to people giving him titbits. I am sure that he will really hurt someone one day, but it seems to be a difficult habit to correct, although I do smack him hard if he tries to nip.

A. Feeding titbits quickly leads to horses and ponies becoming bad tempered if an expected treat is withheld. For this reason, put a notice up outside his box, requesting that titbits are not given, since they make him irritable, and explain it clearly to anyone you catch ignoring the sign. Since he has already started nipping, you will have to either muzzle him or put a grille up on his stable door, so that he cannot actually grab people as they walk past.

Q. I am going to buy a stable soon, but what size should I get?

A. The size of your horse or pony will determine the size of stable that you want. Too small a box will discourage him from lying down, whilst too big an area may encourage him to roll, which could result in him becoming 'cast' (his feet getting trapped against the wall so that he is unable to rise). The following interior dimensions would be about right:

14.2hh and under	10' x 12' approx
14.2hh – 15.2hh	12' x 12' approx
over 15.2hh	12' x 14' approx

Q. My pony keeps barging out of his stable every time I open the door – I just don't seem to be able to stop him from getting past me.

A.   This is a case of bad manners; your pony obviously does not have much respect for your authority. Try to be a little more positive when handling him generally, so that he feels less inclined to push his luck. You will need to be very careful in the way in which you enter his box, too. If there are two bolts on the bottom door, always undo the bottom bolt first – if you leave it until last and he rushes out, you could get a nasty bang on the head. If the stable opens into a yard, close all the gates before attempting to enter anyway. Do not invite trouble by throwing the door wide open, or leaving your pony untied whilst mucking out. Only open the door as wide as is necessary for you to get inside until you can get a headcollar on and tie him up. Once inside, never leave the door ajar anyway, but

Fig. 21. A breast bar.

bolt it securely behind you. Not only do you need to be quick about getting inside, but if necessary be ready to give him a good smack if he tries to push you aside. When you have time, make a minor adjustment to the stable, by adding a breastbar, which can be slid through a staple set on either side of the doorway on the inside. This should be of fairly solid wood, and can be left in place at all times, except when you are actually leading him in and out of the stable. This is also a pleasant way in the summer of keeping the stable cooler, since the bottom door can be left open.

Q. My horse has started kicking his stable door, and is driving everyone mad with the noise. What can be done about it?

A. Part of the problem could be due to boredom – so make sure that he is turned out as much as possible. If you are able to, swap stables with someone, so that he is also positioned in a part of the yard where there is plenty to look at. Provide him with a haynet with smaller holes, so that it takes him longer to eat up his hay, and perhaps give a whole turnip occasionally so that he has something else to nibble at and keep him occupied. He may well be worse at certain times, such as feedtime, if he gets impatient, so have everything ready, rather than making him wait. Some horses do begin to enjoy the sound they make after a while, and whatever diversions you provide, it can be difficult to get this type to stop. Pad the interior with old carpeting or coconut matting as this will both deaden the sound and protect his legs.

Q. My mare is very headshy, and nervous of going into her stable, although the doorway is both wide and high. It is getting very time-consuming to persuade her to go in, and sometimes we have to give up and leave her out. I am reluctant to use force; we tried smacking her once, but she got so worked up she became almost impossible. Are there any other, less time-consuming ways of getting her in, other than by bribery?

A. You might try putting a towel or jacket over her head so that she cannot see where she is going, and reversing her into the stable – you will need to be very careful that she does not bang her hips on the door frame. If this does not work, you will have to go back to bribery and coaxing, or else resign yourself to keeping her out all the year round. If you become really stuck, a field shelter which can have a couple of slip rails

Fig. 22. Reversing into a stable.

put across the entrance may be the only other solution for giving her some extra shelter in the winter.

Q. I keep my pony out all the year round, but as he is very attached to the other pony he lives with, and jumps out of the field if left on his own, I have to stable him for a few hours occasionally. The trouble is, that he tries to climb out over the bottom door; if I close the top one he just kicks and kicks at the walls. How can I keep him in, if I can't close the top door?

Fig. 23. A hole in the stable door to prevent escape and weaving.

A.   He is probably annoyed at not being able to see out, or perhaps a bit claustrophobic. Fit a grid instead – he will still be able to see out, but not get out. Alternatively, cut an oval shaped hole in the top door, and then close it; he will still be able to put his head through the hole, but he won't be able to squeeze himself through.

Q.   My horse has learnt how to undo the top bolt of his stable door and let himself out – how can I stop him before he escapes onto a road?

A.   Putting a leadrope clip onto the bolt as many people do, is not really the answer, as these can still be undone, and can get caught on a lip. Make sure there is a bottom bolt – a kick bolt is best – and invest in a 'pony proof' bolt for the top one. This has a plate incorporated into it which makes it impossible for anyone other than a human to open it. Do not be tempted to padlock him in, as this could be very dangerous in the event of a fire.

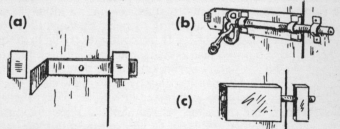

Fig. 24. Door bolts:
(a) A kick bolt operated by foot, suitable as a bottom bolt. (b) A trigger clip to prevent the horse from drawing the bolt back. (c) An enclosed pony proof bolt.

Q.   My horse paws at the ground just in front of the stable door. This is beginning to make a dent in the concrete, and wears the toes on his front shoes very quickly. Is there any way of making him stop?

A.   Boredom often accounts for many of these habits, so try to give him as much as possible to keep his mind occupied. Put a rubber mat down just in front of the stable door, as this will deaden the sound, and save a lot of wear and tear on his shoes. You can find heavy mats of this type advertised in horse magazines.

Q. My horse is always eating her bedding, and gets very fat because of this. Even if I put her fresh straw in last thing at night, she has eaten most of it by next morning, and is standing on exposed concrete. I can't afford to keep on using straw at this rate, and she is so fat I am almost ashamed of her.

A. Being overweight is bad for all horses and ponies, and whilst stabling for part of the day is one way of restricting the food intake, it is not going to be a great success unless you can stop her eating her bed. See if you can find a small, bare paddock, or even a cattle yard where she can wander around; it is more natural than standing in a stable for hours on end, and she may be happier and less inclined to pick at her bedding when she is stabled again.

If there is no alternative but to keep her stabled, or she is so greedy that nothing is going to stop her from wolfing it down, you will need to find ways of discouraging her. Straw eaten in large quantities can irritate the gut or cause a blockage. If she lies down on insufficient bedding she could easily injure herself, and might become reluctant to stale, leading to kidney complaints. Try changing her bedding to peat, shavings or newspaper, which are less tempting. If she continues trying to nibble at these, it could prove just as dangerous in the long run, and the bed should be lightly sprinkled with a diluted non-toxic disinfectant which will give it a slightly unpleasant taste. Fresh bedding should always be well mixed in with the older, slightly soiled bedding for the same reason. Should these measures prove ineffective, you will have no choice but to muzzle her.

Q. My muckheap seems to be permanently out of control. It spreads all over the place – is there some method of keeping it tidy?

A. It helps to keep it in place if you build three retaining walls from breeze blocks, which then only leaves you one side to keep tidy. Jump on it regularly to keep it well packed down; this will help to generate more heat so that it rots down quicker. The heat will also help to destroy any worm eggs in the droppings. The other alternative is to do away with a muckheap altogether, and muck out directly into plastic sacks. These can then be placed in a tidy pile, the tops tied with string, ready to sell or give away to neighbours for their gardens.

Q. My horse has started chewing the wood in his stable; how can I stop him?

A. Creosote all wooden surfaces thoroughly. This will not only preserve them, but give them an unpleasant bitter taste. Make sure that everything has dried completely before putting your horse back in, as creosote can blister. If he starts to chew again, cover the areas with Cribox; although messy, it will stop him. He may be chewing because of a lack in his diet, so add a mineral and vitamin supplement to his short feeds each day.

Q. I have noticed that my horse often stands at his stable door, swaying from side to side. What is this, and why does he do it?

A. This habit is known as 'weaving' and is usually the result of boredom, often combined with a highly-strung temperament. Try to achieve a regular routine so that your horse does not become over-anxious, and turn him out as often as possible, so that he is less likely to get bored. Weaving can lead to a loss of condition, poor digestion, and damage the legs and feet, so you should do all you can to prevent it. Do keep him stabled away from other horses if possible, and away from youngsters, as they often tend to imitate. Fit some kind of anti-weaving grid to his door; preferably the sort which allows him to look out, although not to weave. A full grid which stops him from putting his head over the bottom door will often encourage him to start weaving at the back of the box, rather than to break the habit. (See Fig. 23, pg 64.)

Q. Sometimes my horse takes hold of his stable door with his top teeth, and I notice him swallowing and making an odd sound. Is he in pain, or is this a normal thing?

A. Give him plenty to keep him occupied; like most stable vices, 'crib biting' as it is called is often due to boredom. Once

(a)   **(b)**

Fig. 25.
(a) A fitted crib strap.
(b) A crib strap.

the habit is established, it is quite difficult to break, and it is not unknown for a horse turned out in a field to stand crib biting on the fence rather than grazing. It can also lead to 'wind sucking' which is when the animal learns how to swallow air without having to hold onto anything, and so just applying Cribox to projecting surfaces is not enough. You will need to put a crib strap of some kind on; the type made with a shaped aluminium hinge is usually most successful. This prevents him from arching his neck and swallowing air in the manner you describe. Swallowing air like this can lead to colic and to poor digestion, so it is worth taking some preventive measures.

Q.   How do I go about starting a deep litter bed?

A.   Instead of taking out all the soiled bedding each day, just pick out the droppings, and the worst of the wet stuff. Add fresh bedding to the top, taking care not to mix the bottom layer with the new that you are putting in. Although this can be a very time-saving way of mucking out, and makes a warm winter bed, it must be skipped out, ie the droppings removed regularly, and is not ideal for horses who suffer from thrush. It will also be likely to rot the wooden boards around the edges of the box. The entire bed should be removed completely every six months, the stable disinfected thoroughly, and any wooden boards creosoted.

7

Feeding

Q. Is it really necessary to feed a supplement – surely horses and ponies get all they require by way of minerals and vitamins from their diets?

A.   Feeding a supplement is a way of ensuring that a horse or pony receives all the nutrients he needs. Mineral salts are vital to the biological processes which take place in the body, and are continually being lost through sweating, in the urine and droppings. In the wild they would normally be replaced since the horse would have access to unlimited areas; but since most domesticated animals are restricted to comparatively small areas of grazing, or are stabled, these minerals and vitamins need to be artificially added to the diet. Often the normal diet is not entirely sufficient to meet the horse's needs, since modern agricultural methods have meant that hay and cereals contain lower levels of these nutrients than in the past. Deficiencies can build up over a number of years, and can result in more serious effects; symptoms of deficiencies are when the animal is seen to start stripping bark off trees, eating the soil, or even his own droppings. He is simply trying to find a supply of the nutrients he is lacking.

When feeding a supplement, it is far easiest to buy one which is ready balanced and prepared for your horse and the type of work which he is going to be doing; if you are unsure as to which type of supplement is most suitable, the manufacturers should be able to give you some advice. Some of the 'complete' feeds such as coarse mixes and cubes, already contain amounts of vitamins and minerals, and so if feeding these in some proportion, the amount of supplement given will need to be adjusted accordingly. Once again, if you are unsure as to how much should be given to make up a fully balanced diet, then you should consult the manufacturer – most are very helpful.

The other alternative to actually adding a measured amount of supplement to the diet is to provide a lick of some kind to which the horse can help himself. This can be left in the feed manger, or hung up in the stable or field. Keep an eye on your horse when using it however, as some horses tend to just crunch their way through. In that case it would be wisest to return to adding supplement to the feeds, or else removing the lick for part of the day. Too much is as bad as too little – and unnecessarily expensive.

Q.   I have been told that I should add some salt to my horse's feed each day – yet I have also heard that eating salt is harmful to humans. Surely the same applies to horses as well?

A.   Often it is not the type of food eaten by humans which is detrimental to the health, simply the quantity of it. Overindulgence of anything is bound to be harmful eventually. A small amount of salt added to the diet daily is not going to do much harm when considering the size and bulk of a horse as compared to a human – and it does have its benefits. It is important in the digestive processes, helps to replace salt lost through sweating (sweat is far more concentrated in horses than in humans) and creates a less acidic environment in the stomach, thereby making it less hospitable to worms. When feeding a diet high in oats, it also helps to combat the decalcifying effect they have; for this same reason, the Scots traditionally eat salt with their porridge rather than sugar and cream. Buy a lump of rock salt, and your horse will be able to help himself to what he needs.

Q.   My horse eats his feeds really quickly and I am sure this doesn't do him any good. How can I make him eat more slowly?

A.   He will not get as much benefit from his feeds if he is not chewing them properly; the gastric juices will not be able to work on them as easily, and he may get colic. Do not feed him in a situation where he feels he has to gobble his feed quickly before someone else takes it away from him; if possible, feed

(a)    **(b)**

Fig. 26.
(a) A salt lick holder.
(b) Salt licks threaded with rope.

him well away from other horses and ponies likely to chase him off (he will still feel this even if you are near him) and preferably where he has peace and quiet on his own. Add some chaff to his feeds so he has to chew more thoroughly, and break up a lump of rock salt into large pieces, which can be left in his feed bowl – it will help to slow him down, and this type of salt is so hard that he will not be able to crunch his way through it.

Q. My husband saves grass cuttings from the lawn for my horse, but a friend told me this could be dangerous – is this true?

A. Lawn mowings are best disposed of by making them into a compost heap at the bottom of your garden rather than feeding them to your horse. They could easily choke him, or pack down into a solid mass in the stomach, causing a blockage of the gut. In this state they are likely to ferment, and the gases given off by this process might cause a fatal rupture. Added to this, they could well prove toxic if oil has dripped onto them from the mower, or if poisonous plants have been picked up, or a lawn treatment used.

Q. How much should I feed my horse?

A. This depends upon several factors, one of the most important of which is size. You should work out your horse's weight (height is not a good guide as to weight, since build varies so much). You can do this by either using a special tape measure available from most saddlers, or for an accurate guide, by taking your horse along to the nearest public weighbridge. Alternatively, you might try working out the following equation, although it will give you only a rough estimate:

$$\frac{girth^2 \text{ (in inches)} \times \text{length between pt. of shoulder and pt. of buttock (in inches)}}{290}$$

This will give you an approximate weight in pounds, on which to base your calculations. Generally speaking, you should feed 2 lbs for every 100 lbs bodyweight, although horses in very hard work may need slightly more than this, whilst ponies, or animals with some native blood may be very thrifty and require rather less. How much of this amount you then divide up into a concentrate ration, and how much is fed as roughage and forage (hay and grazing) depends upon the type of work done. As a rough guide, try to work it out along the following lines:

	Concentrates	Roughage, forage
light work	25%	75%
medium work	50%	50%
heavy work	75%	25%

The amount of bulk received should never drop beneath 25% of the total ration, since it is essential in keeping the digestive system working correctly. It is also important to observe the horse's condition carefully; if he becomes overweight or appears too lean, the diet should be adjusted accordingly, both in proportion and content. To a large extent, good feeding depends upon the owner's observation, judgment and 'feel' for the situation, together with a little trial and error until the right formula for the individual animal has been found.

Q. *My horse seems to eat his hay very quickly. As he tends to get fat very easily, I have to keep him stabled quite a lot, and cannot give him much to eat – yet once he has finished his hay he must get very bored.*

A. The solution to this problem is to put the hay in a net which has smaller holes. Do make sure that it is securely fixed however, since if it is pulled down during the night he could injure himself badly if he got tangled up in it. It should also be fastened high enough up to prevent him from getting a foot caught up. You might also provide him with a turnip which will keep him amused once he has finished his net. Bore a hole through the centre of a large whole turnip, and thread a piece of rope through it, and hang up in the stable somewhere. He will not be able to eat it all at once if hung up like this, but it will give him something to nibble at and keep him occupied, without being over-fattening.

Q. *My horse is really difficult to keep weight on, which isn't helped by the fact that he is also a fussy feeder. What can I do about this?*

A. Just as some people are able to eat as many cream cakes and bars of chocolate as they like and never put on any weight, so some horses are similar. This can be very worrying for the owner though. Do check that he is regularly wormed, and that his teeth are not sharp, as both these could contribute to the lack of condition. It might also be a wise precaution to get the vet to give him a blood test to ensure that there is no other reason; he could take a sample of droppings at the same time for a worm count. Consider the diet itself too; it should be of the best quality, see that he has ad lib hay whenever stabled, and peace and quiet in which to eat and digest each feed. Small feeds often are better than one or two large feeds; not only will digestion be more thorough, but it is less off-putting to the fussy feeder. There are also plenty of things you can add to the feeds, both to make them more tempting and to help put some weight on.

Sugar beet pulp: This can be bought in either pulp or cube form; the former must be soaked for at least 12 hours, or until it will absorb no more water, whilst cubes, being more compact, require around 24 hours. It is highly dangerous if fed unsoaked, since it will swell in the gut and cause a blockage. Soak in plenty of water, since it will absorb around three times its own volume. Although it is the dried and crushed remains of sugar beet once the sugar has been extracted, it still contains quite a high proportion of sugar which makes it very palatable. A maximum of 6 lbs (soaked weight) may be fed each day, but in practice, around 2 lbs is usually sufficient, due to its slightly laxative nature. Overfeeding can lead to scouring, but experience will show how much each individual can take. Care must be exercised in its preparation during the summer, when the heat is likely to make it ferment and unsafe to feed.

Carrots: Sliced lengthways (not across which can lead to choking) and added to the feed, these can encourage a fussy feeder to eat up.

Molasses: Molasses, or black treacle, can be added to sweeten a feed, or make a mash more tempting, and is fairly safe to feed. It should be diluted first in order to mix it in; 1 part of molasses to 5 of water. Along the same lines, honey can be used instead, but is rather more expensive to buy.

Eggs: One or two of these can be added to the feed, and will also help to put a bloom on the coat.

Linseed: This can be fed either as an oil (available from the saddler or feed-merchants) or, more beneficially, as a jelly. The seeds are small and brown, and in their uncooked state are highly toxic since they contain prussic acid. They have a high fat content which is easily absorbed by the horse's body, and so are excellent for helping to improve the condition and coat. It should be cooked by placing 20 parts of water to 1 part of linseeds in a sturdy pan and leaving in soak overnight, or for at least 6 hours. After this, the water should be strained off and replaced with fresh, brought to the boil and then simmered uncovered for four hours, or until the seeds have cracked, and it forms a jelly like substance. It needs to be stirred occasionally, and if allowed to boil over can make a terrible smell and mess, so keep an eye on it! About a teacupful when cooked can be added to the feed each day, but should not be fed in combination with chaff.

Stout: Dark beers such as Mackeson's or Guinness, are useful for fattening horses up, and also as a tonic for those which are recuperating after an illness.

Q. I am about to buy a horse, but am unsure as to what I should feed it. Lots of my friends mix up their own feeds and have offered advice, whilst several others recommended that I buy a complete feed. Which is best?

A. Many people like to make up their own mixture of different types of cereals, since it can be easily adjusted to specific requirements, and everything that has gone into it is known. However, those with limited time or storage space often prefer 'complete' feeds – coarse mixes, cubes and so forth, which have been especially mixed at the factory so as to provide an instant, balanced diet, without the need to add anything else other than hay. If you choose the latter method, you should make sure that you choose the right type of feed to suit your horse and the type of work it is expected to do; if in any doubt either the manufacturer or feed merchant should be able to advise you. For the one horse owner, sometimes this can prove to be the cheapest method of feeding, as well as the handiest, since there is likely to be less danger of feed going off before it can be used up. In any event, you ought to check with the previous owner, and find out as to what the horse is used to receiving; there may be certain types of feedstuff which do not suit him for some reason, and it will enable you to avoid upsetting his system by making any sudden changes.

If you wish to change to a different system of feeding, or to introduce a different feedstuff, try to make such alterations as gradual as possible, over a period of weeks, otherwise colic can occur. When opting to mix up your own feeds from different cereals, it helps if you know something of each before deciding upon the quantities you will use.

Here are a few brief guidelines:

Oats: Probably the best balanced of all the grains as they contain the correct proportions of protein, carbohydrates and fats. They should be fed crushed or bruised, rather than whole, for better digestion. They can prove to be rather 'heating' for some animals – that is to say, they may make some horses and ponies over-excitable and difficult to handle.

Barley: This may be bought rolled, or cooked and flaked (often referred to now as micronised barley). This can be a useful substitute for a horse which gets a bit above itself on oats. It is also higher in fats than oats, and so a useful feed for helping to put weight on a poor doer. Overfed it can cause, or aggravate, skin disorders. Rolled barley also shows a tendency to build up fatty tissue around the heart, so is not ideal for a horse in fast work, although flaked and toasted barley is not so bad in this respect. Whole barley cooked together with linseed makes a good additive to the feed of horses who are in poor condition.

Maize: This is a very heating feed, and can lead to laminitis if fed in quantity, especially in ponies. If used, only small quantities should be given (a maximum of 2 lbs) and it should be introduced very gradually to the diet. It is normally bought cooked and flaked.

Bran: This is used as a 'filler' to add bulk to the feed, or it can be fed as a laxative in the form of a mash the evening before a rest day. It should be bought as 'broad' bran, and preferably not fed to young stock as it can have adverse effects on bone growth. Neither should it be fed dry, as it can cause choking.

Chaff: This is useful as a means of providing bulk and fibre in the feed, and encourages proper mastication. Molassed chaff is very palatable to most horses and ponies.

Q. How do I make a bran mash?

A.   Place 3 – 4 lbs of broad bran in the bottom of a bucket, add a good handful of Epsom salts and 3 pints of boiling water. Stir thoroughly with a stick, so that it is of a crumbly mixture, and cover with a piece of old sacking and leave to stand for half an hour. Do check the temperature before feeding, as bran holds the heat well, and it may be a bit hot.

Q. What succulents can I feed my horse other than turnips and carrots?

A.   Especially in the winter, when greenstuff is more scarce, your horse will appreciate some succulents; it is also a way of tempting a fussy feeder, and of preventing boredom in the stabled horse. Turnips can be fed whole, carrots sliced lengthways to prevent choking, plus apples, molasses, parsnips, sugar beet, swede, cabbage, mangolds, kale, grass (either grazed, or long grass scythed and fed fresh) pears, plums (preferably without stones). In some parts of the world, pumpkins are fed, whilst in the East, some horses are given dates.

Q.   I understand that bad feeding can cause colic – what sort of things does this include?

A.   A number of things can cause colic, but bad stable management and feeding are the most frequent factors. This includes:
Working too soon after a feed – at least one hour should be left after the feed has been eaten before commencing exercise. This is because the greatest muscular strain takes place during this first hour; during the second the gastric juices get to work before the food passes into the gut from the stomach.
Over-rich grass – or if the horse is unaccustomed to grazing. Changes in routine must be made slowly.
Sudden changes of diet
Poor quality feed
Bolting feed
Poisonous plants
Feeding a hot horse, or watering a hot horse
Irregular feeding
Drinking after feeding – many horses will sip at their water whilst eating their feed, and this in itself does not normally cause problems. However, if the horse takes a long drink after the feed, it will wash the feed out of the stomach and into the gut, causing poor digestion and possible colic.
Too much feed at once – no feed should be larger than 4lbs in weight as the stomach is comparatively small in horses and cannot cope with more.
Giving hay after a feed – this will push the feed through the stomach, and it may block the gut.
Other causes of colic are: worms, watering a hot horse, sharp teeth, windsucking, crib biting, eating bedding, sand in the stomach, stagnant water, stones in the kidneys, infection in the alimentary canal.

8

Grooming and Clipping

Q. My horse's tail is very wispy and thin, so that it never looks attractive at shows – it has been like this ever since I bought him nearly two years ago. Is there anything I can do to improve its appearance?

A. Not all horses are blessed with thick, luxuriant tails and a wispy one can sometimes look pretty awful, as well as being much less effective as a fly swatter during the summer months. The best thing to do is to stop using a brush on it at all, and to just tease the tangles out very carefully with your fingers so that the hairs aren't broken off. Only use a brush when preparing for a show, making sure that the tail is clean first, and then using only a very soft brush. Put a little baby oil on the brush before use, as this will help to prevent it from pulling at the hairs, and will keep the tail more tangle free in the future. It sometimes helps if you use a conditioner for dry hair after shampooing it, as this type of tail is usually rather brittle haired. To improve the appearance further when showing, divide the tail into three sections whilst it is still damp after washing, and plait down its length, securing the end with an elastic band. When the tail is dry, this will give it a slightly wavy appearance, making it look much fuller than it really is, particularly if the end is also trimmed off level.

Q. I'm having problems with my horse's mane; it is really thick, and although I've tried laying it over with a damp water brush, it doesn't seem to make much difference – it still sticks up in the air!

A. Some manes do grow very thickly, especially in horses or ponies with a certain amount of native blood, or those who have previously been hogged. Keep the mane properly pulled first of all, removing a few hairs at a time from the underside, aiming not just at shortening it, but thinning it out too. Don't attempt to do too much all in one go either, or your horse is likely to get sore, and will rub, making the situation even worse.

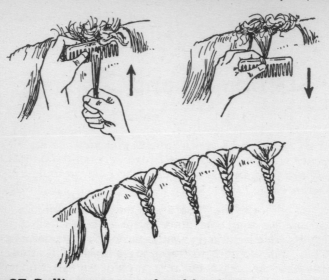

Fig. 27. Pulling mane and stable plaits.

Then lay the mane over with a damp water brush, and put in some loose stable plaits, securing the ends with elastic bands. These can be left in for one or two days, and will help to train the mane to stay on one side rather than sticking up. Always dampen the mane down each time you groom anyway, and pop the plaits back in when the mane starts to get rebellious again.

Q. My horse is quite cobby, and has got very heavy feathering, which makes his legs look like tree trunks. What is the best way of trimming them up?

A.   If you are handy with clippers and have a set at your disposal, you can get quite a neat effect. However, they need to be used carefully, since they sometimes cut a little too closely, giving a two-tone appearance which can look a little odd if the legs are coarsely haired. If you don't have your own set of clippers, can't borrow any, and don't wish to have to pay someone else to perform this service for you, try using scissors instead. You can achieve a tidy result using them in combination with a trimming comb. The advantages over clipping are that you can easily do it yourself at no extra cost, and you are less likely to make the hair at the back of the tendons too short, although it does require a little time and patience. Run the

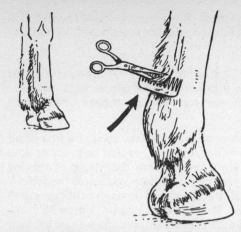

Fig. 28. Trimming legs with a comb and scissors.

comb upwards against the natural lie of the hair, and trim off any hairs which poke through between the teeth with a sharp pair of scissors. Keep repeating the process of backcombing and trimming until you have removed all the excess hair in the areas you want. Don't rush the job, or try to manage without a comb, or you will end up with a series of unsightly ridges leaving the legs looking as though they have been chewed! For the finishing touch, trim around the coronary band as well. The feathers normally act as a 'drainpipe', leading water down the back of the leg and away from the heels, so once you have removed them, you should be sure to pay especial attention to the tender skin in this area, drying it thoroughly when wet, and checking regularly for skin conditions such as cracked heels.

Q.   However many times I wash it, my grey gelding's tail still has a yellowish tinge. How can I make it look white again?

A.   When shampooing the tail, use a biological washing powder, and you will be surprised at the difference it makes. Be careful to only use it on the hairs of the tail however, and not to use it on the dock in case it irritates the skin and makes him rub. Use a conditioner afterwards, and when giving the final rinse, add a sachet of blue bag to the water, which will give a really dazzling blue white finish; these are available from most supermarkets and grocery shops, and cost only a few pence. Finally, once the tail is dry, put some baby oil onto a body brush and go through the tail thoroughly with it. The baby oil will coat the hairs, and help to stop them from getting so dirty again.

Q. I am having a lot of trouble picking up my two year old pony's feet. Not only is it difficult to get him to pick each one up, but once he has, he inevitably slams it back down again before I am ready.

A.   You will find it easier to pick his feet up if you first of all make sure that he is standing squarely, so that he is better able to balance himself. Slide a hand down the inside of the leg which you wish him to pick up, and when you reach the fetlock joint, grasp it firmly, and either click to him or give the command 'Up!' Should he resist, lean gently against him with your shoulder, so that he is encouraged to take his weight off that particular foot, and pinch the base of the tendon, just above the fetlock joint, between thumb and forefinger as well. Do remember that youngsters tend to be rather unco-ordinated, and he may find it difficult to lift his feet up very high, or to keep his balance on three legs for very long, so make sure that you are not being over-demanding in this respect. If he is not genuinely losing his balance though, and is persisting in this habit out of sheer naughtiness, you must put your own foot down firmly, and reprimand him sharply, accompanied by a smack if necessary.

Q. I thought I'd pull my pony's mane the other day as it is getting very long. When I started, he wasn't too badly behaved at all, but after a bit he started getting very irritable, swinging his quarters around so that he squashed me against the wall, and throwing his head about. He has been just as bad ever since – how on earth can I make him behave so that I can finish his mane off?

A.   Some horses and ponies are more sensitive than others when it comes to mane and tail pulling, and if you try to do too much in one go, they will become very sore, making them bad tempered and also inclined to rub, spoiling all your efforts. Rather than doing a lot at once, just attempt a little each day, preferably after exercise when he is warm, and the hairs will come out more easily. Select the longest hairs from the under-side of the mane, using a trimming comb to backcomb and separate them. Wrap the hairs once around the comb, or place

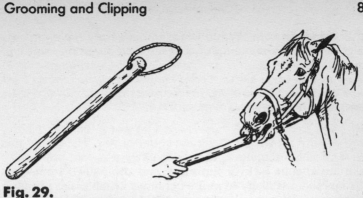

Fig. 29.
(a) A home-made twitch
(b) A twitch when put on.

your thumb firmly on top of them, and pull downwards so that they come out from the roots rather than breaking. Make sure that you take hold of only a few hairs at a time, pulling them out quickly and sharply rather than tugging on them, which will be painful. Tail pulling follows a similar technique; start at the top of the dock, selecting the longest hairs from the bottom and sides, and working your way downwards. If he is terribly unco-operative, you may need to resort to getting someone to hold him, and put a twitch on, but it is best to persevere for a while with this more tactful approach in order to avoid creating a mental hang up about it all.

Q. My horse will let me groom all of his head without fuss, except for his left ear. As far as I can see, there does not seem to be any real reason for this, and it is becoming quite a nuisance.

A. Since your horse does not object to the rest of his head being groomed, just one ear, it sounds likely that there is something wrong with it, and it is not just due to naughtiness. It is always best not to jump to conclusions, and if it is difficult just touching this ear, then it is unlikely that you have been able to give it a really thorough inspection. He could be suffering from an ear infection, mites, or even have a hay seed stuck in it, which would cause a lot of discomfort, and explain his behaviour. The best thing to do is to call the vet and get him to check it properly, since many of these problems are not immediately visible, and it will certainly take the two of you to get a better look.

Q. I have lost confidence when grooming my mare. All she does is try and snap and occasionally kick out at me, so I end up grooming her as little as possible. Is there anything I can do to try and improve her temper? I really dread grooming as I am sure I will get hurt one day. Otherwise she is excellent to ride, so I don't really want to part with her.

A.   The fear of getting hurt is often far worse than the reality, and you are allowing it to get the better of you. The longer this state of mind continues, the more likely it is that your mare will sense your lack of authority and confidence from your actions and it is likely to make her more irritable and prone to playing up. You will simply have to take a deep breath and go in and get on with it – you cannot skimp on grooming since it could affect her health eventually. Stay fairly close to her, so that should she try to kick out she will only succeed in pushing you away from her. If you stand too far away she is far more likely to inflict serious damage. Tie her up fairly short, so that she can't reach to nip or bite and be firm, speaking sharply to her and give her a smack as well if necessary if she starts to misbehave. The chances are that with a more positive attitude. she will soon pack this game in, but you must first of all make a stand and let her know that she isn't going to get away with it or else she will never have any respect for you.

If it helps to make you feel a bit more confident, try putting a muzzle on when grooming, so you know that she cannot possibly bite you – it is not really as horrid as it sounds. A plastic bucket type is fairly cheap and obtainable from your saddler, but make sure it fits properly as they can sometimes rub. Your saddler will be able to advise you on the fit if you are uncertain. Take care not to aggravate the situation since mares are often more sensitive than geldings, particularly when they are in season. Do not use stiff brushes on her more ticklish spots – under the belly, between the front and back legs, and around the flanks, are the areas to be most careful of. Use a soft brush instead, firmly but patiently. When dirt and sweat are caked on, you may even find it easier to wash these places with warm water, and towel them dry afterwards. Try not to be abrupt in your movements either, but talk quietly to her as you work, since you will find that it helps steady your nerves quite as much as it soothes her.

Q.   I enter one or two local showing classes whenever there is a show near to us, and a lot of people have told me that I should

*trim my horse's whiskers off for these – is this cruel? If I do
decide to trim them off, how can I do this most neatly?*

A.   Trimming off the whiskers can improve the appearance
tremendously, making a coarse head look more refined,
especially if the jawline and ears are done at the same time.
The hairs on the muzzle are simply 'feelers' to help the horse
pick out its food when grazing. It is not cruel to cut them off,
and is not at all painful, and he will manage quite easily without
them; should you change your mind they will grow back very
quickly in any case. You can either trim them off very carefully
using a pair of scissors, or for a quicker and neater result use
a disposable ladies' safety razor instead. It is best to do this on

**Fig. 30. Holding an ear pressed together and
trimming round the edge.**

the morning of a show so that you don't end up with a light
growth of stubble. The jawline can be trimmed up using scissors,
as can the ears. When trimming the latter, press the edges close
together and cut along the edges, but do not actually remove
the hairs from the inside, as they are functional in helping to
prevent particles of dirt from getting inside.

*Q.   I've got a three year old gelding which I hope to help break
in soon. At the moment I handle him as much as possible,
teaching him to stand, lead, pick up his feet and so on. The
trouble is that he has started to nip quite a lot – am I right in
smacking him or will he grow out of this when he has finished
teething? He also chews everything around, including his leadrope when he is tied up, which I assume is related to this problem.*

A.   You must certainly smack him for nipping, which may be
partly due to teething, but is nonetheless inexcusable behaviour.
He must learn to respect you, and discover that he cannot get
away with this or any other unsociable habits, or it could turn

into an unpleasant and painful vice. Growl at him at the same time, and you will find that eventually he will understand your disapproval of his actions without your necessarily always having to give him a smack as well. At this age you really will have to assert your authority, or you could have real problems later on if he comes to consider you merely one of the herd, instead of the boss.

You will have to keep grooming kit and so forth out of temptation's way in order to stop them being chewed, and give wooden surfaces a coat of Cribox (available from your saddler) or creosote to give them an unpleasant taste, or else your horse will develop an expensive habit impossible to break once it is established. When you need to tie him up, use a rack chain rather than a leadrope; these are made from steel, which he will not be able to chew through. It consists of a central ring with an 18″ length of chain on either side, and terminating in a spring clip at each end. It should however, be looped through a piece of string which will break in an emergency, rather than attached to anything fixed.

Q.   I enjoy taking my horse to shows – the trouble is that he gets so dirty overnight, and is covered in stains the next morning, whether I bring him in or leave him out in the field. This means that I always have to bath him on the morning of the show, which means my getting up very early so that he is dry in time, and tends to take some of the shine off his coat. Is there any way in which I could keep him clean so that I could bath him the day before?

A.   When your horse is dry, bring him into his stable and put a summer sheet on, which will keep most of his body clean if it is fairly deep. Bandage his legs too, as this will help to keep them respectable. Make sure that there is plenty of fresh clean bedding in his stable, and skip it out as late as possible in the evening, so that there is as little as possible to roll in. You will probably find that there will be a few stains in the morning, but it will not take as long to deal with these as to give him a complete bath. If you find it necessary on some occasion to wash all of him, and are worried that he has lost some of the shine on his coat, you could buy some coat gloss from your saddlers which works quite successfully – or if you forget to buy it, a little furniture polish from an aerosol on a stable rubber also will do the trick. A small test patch should be done first though to make sure that there is no allergic reaction, eczema or itchiness.

Q. A lot of books mention that you should wash your horse's sheath regularly – but none of them say how to go about this!

A. Washing the sheath regularly is an important part of grooming, as dirt and dried excreta can accumulate inside making it both uncomfortable and allowing the possibility of infection. Once a week, using warm water, mild soap and a sponge, wash out inside the sheath as far as you can get, rinsing well with clean water afterwards. Keep a separate sponge for this task, rather than using the ones kept for wiping the eyes and dock. Finish off by drying with a clean towel as thoroughly as you are able to, and apply a little Vaseline or baby oil to prevent any soreness. Be careful of sharp fingernails or wearing rings, and be fairly cautious when dealing in this area anyway, as some animals are very ticklish. Just as important a piece of hygiene is to remember to wipe beneath the dock – this again should be lightly oiled with Vaseline or baby oil afterwards to keep it feeling comfortable. Mares should have their udders and vulvas washed just as frequently as a gelding's sheath, if not more frequently since they tend to get dirtier.

Q. I am thinking of getting my horse freezemarked, and wonder if this is likely to affect a judge's opinion when I am showing him. Also, is it at all painful?

A. Freezemarking is an excellent way of deterring thieves and well worth spending the money on. It is almost completely painless: the area marked (usually beneath the saddle) will be slightly swollen for a few days, but you should be able to ride again after a week. The pigmentation of the hair cells is destroyed by the 'branding' process. When new hair starts to grow through again after about twelve weeks it is white in colour, so that the numbers and letters are visible in contrast against the coat. It is possible to freezemark grey or white animals too: the marking irons are simply left on for a slightly longer period of time so that the hair is killed completely and the numbers and letters appear as bald patches instead. It should not affect a judge's decision in the show ring, but if you are worried, another option is to have an invisible 'microchip' inserted in the crest of the neck by your vet.

Q. My horse is really bad about being tied up – he seems to hang back all the time and breaks quite a number of leadropes. When I smack him he only gets more uptight, so how can I stop this habit?

A.   If he was just being naughty, a smack would probably have sorted this out – but it sounds more as though your horse has perhaps had a nasty experience in the past whilst tied up, and obviously panics when he feels restricted. Make sure that you do not give him any cause to hang back by being rough or abrupt whilst working around him. Try hanging up a small

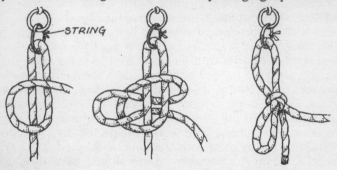

Fig. 31. Stages in the tying of a quick release knot.

haynet to keep him occupied. Always tie him to a piece of string which will break in the event of an emergency, rather than the leadrope or his neck. Use a quick release knot too, which can be easily undone should he become distressed, whilst you go to his head and reassure him. Patience will help to improve matters to a degree, but he is unlikely ever to be totally reliable about being tied up, so you should never leave him tied up on his own without supervision.

Q.   My gelding has a very thick coat, even during the summer. This means that he gets terribly hot when I exercise him and he loses a lot of weight because of it. I clip him in the winter, but would it be all right to do so during the summer months as well?

A.   There is no reason at all why you shouldn't – clipping him out completely sounds as if it would be the most beneficial to him, and it would mean that there were no lines. Check him in the evenings as they are often rather cool by comparison with daytime temperatures, and he may appreciate a rug to keep him warm.

Q.   I would like to clip my horse as I think he would look much smarter. What sort should I choose?

A.   Clipping should be done because it is necessary to do so, not purely to improve a horse or pony's looks. The reasons for clipping are that by removing some of the thick winter coat, he will sweat less heavily and so is more likely to maintain condi-

Fig. 32. Types of clip.

tion, will be capable of more fast work without becoming so distressed, will be less likely to catch a chill since the coat will dry more quickly, and will be easier to keep clean. Clipping may also be necessary to make it easier to treat certain skin diseases.

However, clipping does mean that in most cases you will have to keep him warm when he is not working by putting rugs on to replace the missing coat, and you may even have to stable him as well if you intend clipping very much off. Choose the type of clip according to how you are able to keep him, and your capabilities as a rider. Bear in mind that if he is minus rather a lot of winter coat, stabled and not receiving a great deal of exercise, he will be a rather more lively ride than normal when you do take him out and he starts to feel the cold. A *sweat clip* is quite suitable for a horse living out which does not do a great deal of work; the really tough native types often don't need a rug since very little hair is removed, just a strip from the throat, bottom of the neck, and chest. If he lives out, but will have to work moderately hard, you could try a fairly low *trace clip,* where hair is removed from the throat, lower part of neck, chest, belly, and around the stifle – but a New Zealand rug will be necessary, perhaps even with an extra blanket stitched inside it if the weather is very bad. The rug should be as deep as possible since the belly does get rather cold otherwise, even if only a small amount of hair has been removed.

Consider also the type of work the horse is expected to do. One which is going hunting, for example, should not have its legs clipped out, since the additional hair there will help both to keep it warm when standing still, and to give it some protection against brambles and so forth when on the move. Horses prone to feeling the cold should ideally be left with some hair covering their loins, and those tending to be 'cold backed' will also often benefit from having at least a saddle patch left on. This will also act to a degree as a cushion against soreness if the horse is going to be ridden for long periods.

Provided you are able to keep your horse stabled at nights, you can within reason, choose a clip which will deceive the eye a little and help improve its appearance – provided of course, that it is appropriate to all the conditions mentioned so far. A trace clip can help to make a horse with a short back look a little more proportionate, whilst if its legs are a little short then a high trace clip helps to make them appear a little longer. A *'chaser clip* can make a horse which tends to work on its forehand (ie supports most of its weight over its shoulders) look less so, and a *blanket clip* will help shorten up a horse with a long back. A *full or hunter clip* is really only necessary if your horse is going to be in very hard work. Clipping out the head, or a bridle clip (according to how much of the body hair you are removing) will also help to refine a head which looks rather coarse and hairy in the winter.

Q. My horse is really difficult to clip. I bought a set of clippers with a friend, thinking that in the long term it would work out cheaper than paying someone else to do it. I only bought my horse in the summer, and thought he would be fine about it as he was so good in every other situation. The first time I tried though, he went berserk – I dropped the clippers, and they have just been repaired at great expense. I am now rather wary about another attempt – how can I ensure that he behaves?

A.   Clipping is often the last thing on your mind if you buy a horse during the summer months, but it is always wise to enquire about such things! For the moment, persevere with a gentle approach, as he may have been frightened in the past. Run the clippers near to his stable each day to try and accustom him to the noise. When he seems quite settled about this, try again, making sure that you have an assistant to hold him. You should also take the precaution of slipping your hand through the wrist loop provided on the clippers so that if he panics again you don't end up dropping them. If he still objects, try putting some cotton wool in his ears as some horses simply object to the sound. If this makes no difference, then you may need to get your assistant to twitch him. A twitch may be made by drilling a hole in the end of a piece of sawn-off broom handle, and threading a piece of thin rope or plaited baler twine approximately 24" in length through it, and knotting the ends securely together. This loop is then passed over the horse's top lip, and the piece of handle twisted to tighten it. On removal (which should be frequent) the nose should be rubbed vigorously to restore the circulation. In the event that you have to resort to such measures, it is often best to just clip a little in several sessions rather than attempt to do too much and risk upsetting him even more. He may have been nicked in the past, remember the event and so be nervous now. Provided you don't do the same again you can hope that he will gain in confidence with time. Make sure that the clippers themselves are not at fault. Check that they are correctly earthed so they are not giving him any little shocks, that the blades are sharp enough and the tension correctly adjusted so they do not pull at the hairs, making the whole process unnecessarily painful.

Despite these precautions, you may still find that he is not too keen on the idea, in which case you will have to ask the vet to sedate him. You should still be careful though, and restrict yourself to a reasonably small area, since these injections are not effective for very long, and the horse may start to recover full consciousness with little or no warning. Frequently however, once the horse has been sedated and successfully clipped, it seems to accept it all much better the next time, being better behaved and not always needing sedation first.

Heads can often be a bit tricky with a nervous horse, so you might also find it a good investment to buy either a set of hand clippers or battery/rechargeable clippers of the type often used for dogs. These have smaller heads, are more manoeuvrable and easier to hold, quieter and cause less vibration.

Q. I am taking my pony to be clipped at a local riding school next week. Her previous owners have said that she is fine in this respect so I am not expecting any trouble – but are there any preparations I should make first?

A.   Do make sure your pony is as clean as possible, since dirt and dried sweat clogs the clippers, makes them overheat, blunts the blades, and causes them to pull painfully at the hair. Grease also makes clippers overheat, and is difficult to clip through, so try to remove the worst of it. Without actually giving him a bath you can put a capful of Dettol into half a bucket of warm water, wring out a sponge in it, and then rub it vigorously against the lie of the hair. Rinse it out in the water and repeat. The grease forms a white scum on top of the water. Concentrate on the worst of the greasy areas where your pony is to be clipped, and then dry as well as possible with a towel.

Your pony should be dry when clipped, so, if you are hacking over, or if he gets hot travelling in the trailer, leave some extra time and arrive early so that he can dry off. Take a headcollar, and also a bridle if you are not riding him over there, in case you need some extra control. If you are going to be holding him, wear rubber footwear, and a headscarf or some form of hat – this will stop your hair getting in the way, and will certainly help to prevent your becoming covered with bits of clipped hair! Try and wear a jacket or an old shirt over your clothes too otherwise you will find that the clippings get everywhere, and make you generally uncomfortable.

9

The Foot and Shoeing

Q. My pony is unshod at the moment, and has been since I bought him a couple of months ago. I do very little roadwork, but my friends have all told me that it is cruel to work him without shoes. Is this true?

A. If your pony has been used to working without his shoes for some time, his feet will have become quite tough and hard, in the same way as your own feet become tougher and more leathery if you spend much time barefoot. Provided that you avoid roadwork as much as possible, he should be fine, although when the ground gets very hard and dry in the summer, he may possibly get a little footsore. Otherwise, there is no reason why you should work him with shoes if you do not wish to, but do have the farrier call on a regular basis as his feet will still need trimming to keep them in good shape and prevent any cracking.

Q. My horse seems to slip a lot whenever I ride him on the roads – are there any special shoes which would give him a better grip?

A. Do make sure that a part of this problem is not due to your way of riding. Some roads can be treacherously slippery,

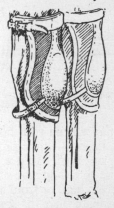

Fig. 33. Fitted knee boots.

so you should keep sufficient rein contact to enable him to remain well balanced, and avoid pushing him on too fast in any gait. On roads which you know are particularly bad, stick to a steady walk if necessary, even if it takes a little longer. It would be a wise investment to buy a pair of knee boots to hack out in, in order to try and protect him against the possibility of an accident. It sounds as though your horse would also benefit tremendously from being shod with road studs or carbide-tipped nails – ask your farrier about this. Make sure that he is regularly shod as well, since worn shoes provide little purchase on such surfaces.

Q. I'm going to start competing in cross country competitions soon – should I use studs in my horse's shoes?

A.   The principle of using studs is similar to that of an athlete wearing spikes in his running shoes. Studs can be handy for all sorts of competitive work, dressage as well as showjumping or cross country riding. They give a better purchase on the ground; consequently the horse gains more confidence in its ability to perform whatever is required of it. They are not an absolute must of course, as many people do compete quite successfully without them. But if you wish to achieve the best possible

Fig. 34. Different types of stud.

performance from your horse, they can give you that extra bit of advantage when the ground conditions are not ideal.

Ask your farrier to put stud holes in your horse's shoes the next time he is shod; you will be able to buy the studs themselves either from him, or from a saddler. Use pointed studs for hard going, square ones for soft going, whilst if it is springy, small studs should be used in all four shoes for dressage, but large dome-shaped ones for jumping and cross country. The choice can be bewildering if you are not familiar with them, so you should ask your farrier or saddler for advice if you are not sure about which you want. When jumping, only put studs in the outside heels of the back shoes, as there is less chance of the rider being injured by the back feet than the front ones in the event of a fall. Similarly, if the studs are in the outside heels, the horse will not injure himself so badly should he accidentally tread on himself.

To put the studs in, you will need a tap, spanner, an old shoeing nail, and the studs you have decided to use. Clean the stud holes out first, using the nail, and then the tap – this has a thread on it the same size as the hole, and will clear the threads and ensure that the stud goes in more easily. Then screw the stud in, using the spanner to tighten it up, and taking care to ensure that it is straight, not at an angle. When the competition is over, remove the studs again unless they are designed to stay there permanently. Competition studs are unsuitable for roadwork and the like, and they will not only cause the horse to work lopsidedly on a hard surface, but are likely to shear off besides. Once you have taken the studs out, insert 'sleepers' which fit flush with the shoes, or else plug the holes with a piece of oiled cotton wool, which will stop grit and dirt from accumulating and clogging up the threads.

Q. When I was picking out my mare's feet the other day, I noticed that there were quite a few ragged pieces of frog hanging off. She is not lame, but will these eventually make her so, or affect her in any way? I haven't noticed them before.

A. This is quite a normal occurrence. The frog and sole of the foot are continuously producing new cells, which are normally worn away through contact with the ground. As this has not happened very effectively with your mare's feet, you should ask your farrier to trim the ragged pieces off next time he calls to shoe. This will not hurt, as it is only dead tissue; but if it is neglected, dirt could become lodged beneath the ragged pieces, and an infection, such as thrush, could arise. It might be a good idea to have a chat with your farrier anyway as the frog may not be wearing away because it is not in contact with the ground when the horse moves. Special shoes may help. The frog should make contact with the ground, as this plays an important part in promoting the circulation of the blood in the feet and legs.

Q.   My farrier won't ever replace the old shoes when he comes to see my gelding – he always insists on putting new ones on. This is very costly – should I say something about it to him, or change to another farrier?

A.   There is probably a very good reason for this; the shoes may look reasonably substantial but might in fact be quite worn, and would not last until the next visit. They could snap across the toes, or the heels wear right through, and they would not afford your horse a great deal of grip either. He will need reshoeing around every four to six weeks. If you do not ride on the roads much, you may be able to get away with using the old set once, but if your activities involve much work on hard surfaces, they wear more quickly, and your farrier is right to recommend a new set. Make sure that your horse is not harder on his shoes than he should be by keeping him active with elevation in the stride. If you notice that he wears the toes of his back shoes out more quickly than his front ones, get your vet to examine him, as it could be a sign of the onset of navicular disease.

Q.   My horse dishes quite badly; is there any corrective shoeing which can be performed to correct this trait?

A.   There is little that can be done about 'dishing' (the front feet swinging outwards as the animal moves). If you try to correct it by shoeing, to change the natural angle of the foot to the ground, you may place strain on the joints and inner structures. If your horse is young, there is a good chance that as he grows older and stronger, the characteristic will lessen.

Q.   I have noticed that my horse is not going so well now that the ground has become so hard. His stride is noticeably shorter and more stilted and he moves far less freely and is hesitant when jumping, which is very unlike him. Could there be something wrong with his shoes?

A.   You should have him examined by the vet in case there is a more deep-seated problem here, although by the sound of it, the hard ground is jarring his legs and feet causing him some discomfort. What he is feeling when he is jumping is similar to the sensation you receive when jumping off a wall with your legs braced, instead of flexing them. As you can imagine, this would become quite painful after a while. Reduce the amount of work you are doing on hard surfaces, even if it does mean having to miss a few shows. It is more important to keep your horse sound for the future than to risk him for the sake of a few rosettes. Whilst the ground remains so hard, it would be best if you could carry out serious schooling and jumping on the more yielding surface of a manege or indoor school. If you enquire locally, you should find that it is possible to hire the use of one at a reasonable price from a nearby riding school or livery yard. Particularly if he is young, you must remember that too much work on hard ground could damage his legs, and even result in permanent unsoundness. Regarding shoeing, have a word with your farrier about the possibility of shoeing him with some form of hoof cushion to absorb some of the concussion.

Q. Due to a hectic work schedule for the next two months I am planning to turn my horse out to grass for a holiday. Should I continue keeping him shod, or have his shoes taken off altogether?

A. If your horse's feet are in good condition, you could remove his shoes altogether if you wish, although they will still need attention from your farrier to keep them right. As it is only a short time, you might feel it is preferable to keep your horse shod; certainly if his hooves are prone to cracking at all, you ought to at least have 'grass tips' put on. There are thin, half-length shoes which will protect the toes where the hoof wall is

Fig. 35. Grass tips.

most susceptible to damage. If he is unused to being turned out, or kicks, then it is always best to leave the back shoes off altogether. Your farrier is probably the best person to consult about your horse's feet, as he will be most familiar with their condition, and so will be able to advise you on the wisest course of action to take.

Q. Is there anything I should do ready for when the farrier arrives to shoe my new horse?

A. If possible, do try to be present when the farrier is shoeing, as he may want you to hold your horse if he is awkward, rather than tying him up. Timewise, this may occasionally be awkward, and so if other people share your grazing, you will find it mutually beneficial to share this chore, since you will then be able to take it in turns to fetch the horses in ready. Make sure that you catch your horse in plenty of time.

If you are unable to be around and nobody else is prepared to bring him in for you, then you will have to leave him stabled, or in a smaller and closer field. The farrier will not appreciate having to tramp across to the far side of a muddy fifty acre field – in fact he is just as likely to turn round and go home in disgust! If you are able to leave him in, then give his feet a good scrub and dry them as well as you are able to, as this will make the job easier and pleasanter. The farrier will probably also appreciate the offer of a cup of tea or coffee; and prompt payment too!

Q. My horse tends to have very dry, brittle feet which crack easily so that he tends to keep losing his shoes. What can be done about this?

A.   Although your horse's feet should not be allowed to become overlong, if he is shod too frequently the hoof wall will become weakened due to the number of holes made by the nails. Have a chat with your farrier to see if it is possible to leave the shoes on a bit longer.

There are certain conditions which are likely to remove the varnish secreted by the perioplic band at the top of the hoof wall. This coats the hoof's walls preventing the evaporation of moisture. Its absence allows the horn to become dry and brittle. These conditions, include working in salty areas (indoor schools and maneges often contain a large quantity of salt to prevent the surface from becoming too dry and dusty), sandy areas, or if the horse is bedded on shavings or sawdust.

The feet should also be washed with cold water and a soft water brush when they become caked with mud, since the grit will also scratch if it is allowed to remain.

Protect the hooves by coating them daily (once they are clean) with one of the many proprietary brands of hoof grease available from the saddler. Try bedding your horse down on peat, as this seems to help promote a stronger, healthier growth. A feed supplement containing biotin or methionine will improve the quality of horn growth from within, although it will take months of continuous use before you see any change.

Q. My horse seems to be particularly prone to bruising her soles, which means that she spends some time off work each time this happens. Is there anything that the farrier could do about this?

A.   Horses with thin, or flat rather than concave soles, tend to be more liable to bruising, which can be rather inconvenient. Ask your farrier if he feels that shoeing with a leather pad or Equicushions would be of benefit. Remember also that corns are another form of bruising, and are likely to lead to lameness. The cause may be small stones becoming wedged between the heel of the shoe and hoof. Perhaps the heels of the shoes are too long or too short. Frequently, the shoes are left on for too long, so do make sure that your horse is shod regularly.

Q.   The other day my farrier commented on the fact that my horse brushes, and suggested that next time he calls he puts on feather edged shoes. What exactly are these?

A.   'Brushing' occurs when the inside of one hoof strikes against the opposite leg. Depending upon the area affected, you should use some protective boots, either brushing boots, fetlock boots, a coronet boot or anti-brushing ring, to prevent injury. You could also follow your farrier's advice and shoe

Fig. 36. Feather edged shoe.

with 'feather edged' shoes so that he does not harm himself so badly when out in the field, or damage his boots too badly. These are shoes which are slightly narrower and set back inwards from the hoof wall along the inside branches, so that if he strikes himself it is only with the horn of the hoof, rather than with the shoe. Fewer nails are used along the inside branch so that the chance of his cutting himself if the clenches have risen are further reduced.

Q.   How can I tell whether my horse is being well shod or not?

A.   One of the most important things is that the shoe has been made to fit the foot, not vice versa. It should also appear to be of the right size and weight for the animal and the type of work which it is expected to do. A heavy shoe is unsuitable for a small pony, whilst too light a one will quickly be worn out by a heavy horse. On close inspection, you should see that the shoe also meets the hoof wall exactly, otherwise dirt and grit can work its way upwards, creating an infection; it will also create an uneven pressure on the weight bearing surfaces of the foot which could result in structural damage. The traditional number of nails used is seven – four on the outside and three on the inside, but fewer may be used if the foot is small, or the walls thin, or the animal is inclined to brush. The nails themselves come in various sizes and are used according to the size of animal being shod. Too large a nail can lead to cracking,

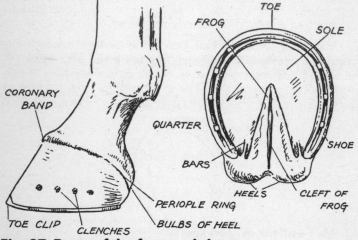

Fig. 37. Parts of the foot and shoe.

whilst too small a nail gives insufficient grip and movement will occur between shoe and hoof, eventually resulting in the shank of the nail breaking and the shoe becoming loose. Look at the nail heads; after shoeing they should lie flush with the shoe if the correct size of nail has been used.

One of the easiest points to check for yourself is the accuracy of the nailing on. If the horse has good feet, the points where the ends of the nails appear through the hoof walls and are turned down to form a hook to hold the shoe in place (the clenches) should be in a straight line, rather than at uneven heights with some lower or higher than others. The height of the clenches should be approximately one third of the way up the wall of the hoof. It is more difficult for the lay person to determine whether the hoof itself is prepared correctly; but the 'bars' of the foot (the parts of the hoof wall which turn inwards towards the frog) should never be cut away, as they have a vital part to play as part of the surface supporting the horse's weight, in absorbing concussion, and helping to return blood from the foot and up the leg. Look at the angle of the foot, and you should be able to note that its slope is the same as that of the pastern. If this line is broken, stresses are then placed unequally, not just within the foot, but the leg as well.

There is not a lot that a farrier can do for a foot which is badly shaped where it is due to hereditary conformation. Here he should shoe to the shape of the foot rather than trying to make it conform to the 'ideal', and the horse is more likely to remain sound.

Watch how your horse is handled; a farrier who is firm but quiet is far more likely to do a good job than one who is abrupt, upsets the horse and then has trouble getting the shoe on because the animal won't stand still.

Your horse should be shod regularly; a farrier cannot be held to blame for a foot in poor condition if you have neglected to call him in the first place! Most farriers are only too pleased to explain a little about their trade and what they are doing if you express an interest in it, so do not be afraid to ask questions.

Q.   What is the best way of removing a shoe if it becomes loose?

A.   If the shoe is very loose, or has twisted so that it is in danger of injuring your horse, you can remove it yourself. Ask your farrier to demonstrate this one day and how to hold up both front and back feet so that you will be well prepared in the event of an emergency. Ask him if he will sell you an old rasp and some pincers – or you could even make do with what you have in the tool box. The easiest way to remove the shoe is to rasp the clenches away first so that you do not pull any of the hoof away as you remove the shoe. Once all of the clenches have been rasped down, place the pincers at the outside heel of the shoe. Get the jaws as far beneath it as you can, and holding them firmly, lever downwards and slightly inwards towards the toe. As the shoe begins to come away, repeat the procedure on the inside heel, then return to the outside and carry on working the shoe off from each side in turn, finishing at the toe.

10

Veterinary Problems

Q. I have a light chestnut pony whose nose gets sunburnt in the summer – it cracks and gets very red and sore. Is there anything I can put on to stop it happening, as it looks most painful?

A. Light coloured horses and ponies, and those with light coloured or pink muzzles can be quite prone to sunburn. Try using a sunblock or chapstick when he is turned out, and put calamine lotion on to help soothe the skin. You might also consider stabling him during the daytime when the sun is at its hottest; the shelter from flies will probably be appreciated as much as the respite from the heat.

Q. Recently I have noticed that my horse is taking longer than usual to eat his feeds, and I sometimes find chewed up bits of hay lying beneath his haynet, as though he has spat it out. Is he being fussy, or could he be feeling unwell?

A. Since your horse is still eating up his feed, it sounds very likely that he is suffering from sharp teeth, which are causing him some discomfort when he is chewing. As a result, he is dropping pieces of half chewed food from his mouth, which will mean that he gets neither his full ration, nor a great deal of benefit from that which he does swallow. It could also be due to other types of mouth ailment; lampas (an inflammation of the soft palate), mouth ulcers, or an abscess. Ask your vet to do a proper check for you. Remember to have your horse's teeth checked every six months anyway, and rasped as needed, since sharp edges could cause lacerations of the tongue and mouth, creating difficulties not only in eating, but when riding too.

Q. A friend had a look at my horse's teeth the other day, and reckoned that he is older than I thought he was. How exactly can you tell the age by looking at the teeth?

A.   It is possible to estimate a horse's age with a reasonable amount of accuracy until it reaches 8 years old, when it is said to be 'aged'. After this, it is a matter of guesswork. Even with a younger animal, you should still bear in mind that all individuals may vary slightly from the given 'pattern' of tooth growth and development. Environment, breeding, feeding, general health and conformation will all play a part in altering the way in which the teeth become worn. The teeth you look at to determine a horse's age are the incisors, or the front teeth which

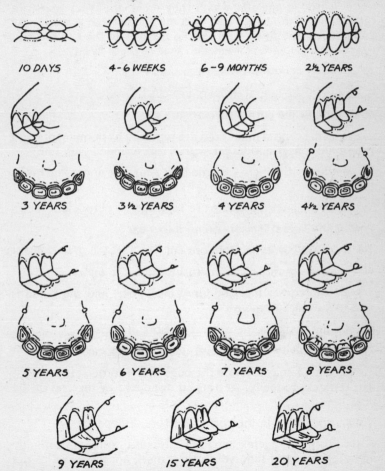

Fig. 38. Stages of ageing in teeth.

are used for biting off grass. There are six of these in each jaw, given the names 'centrals', 'laterals', and 'corners' according to their positions. The surface where the top and bottom sets of teeth meet is referred to as the 'table'; in a younger horse the enamel around the edges of each tooth's table is seen to be higher than the black centres, giving the effect of a shallow cavity. As the animal grows older, so this cavity becomes shallower, until the surfaces of the teeth are flat. The older the horse becomes, the longer the teeth also appear to be, and the more acute the angle at which they meet; the black marks in the centres of the tables also become smaller and rounder. As an approximate guide, you should be able to see the teeth in the following stages of wear and tear at these ages;

10 days two central milk teeth are cut

4 – 6 weeks the lateral incisors are cut

6 – 9 months the corner incisors are cut

2½ years the central milk teeth are replaced by permanent teeth (these are longer and larger with a less rounded gum line)

3 years the central incisors come into wear (the upper and lower teeth meet)

3½ years the lateral incisors are replaced by permanent teeth

4 years the lateral incisors come into wear

4½ years the corner incisors are cut

4½ years the canine teeth or 'tushes' erupt in males

5 years the corner incisors come into wear, and the horse is said to have a 'full mouth'

6 years the cavity in the central incisors disappears

7 years the cavity in the lateral incisors disappears

7 years a hook may form on the edge of the corners; it develops and recedes gradually, starting to disappear by the end of the year

8 years the cavity in the corner incisors disappears

After this point, ageing becomes difficult to estimate with any accuracy; at about nine years old a mark appears close to the gum on the upper corner incisors, and gradually extends downwards. This is called 'Galvayne's groove'. At about fifteen years it extends half way down the length of the tooth, and down the entire length at about twenty years old. After this it gradually disappears, and the only indication of age in an old horse is the length and angle of the teeth, and the wearing of the tables.

Q. My horse has a front tooth missing: is this going to cause problems?

A. Where a tooth has been lost, there will be nothing to wear down the surface of the opposite one, and so you should make sure that it is kept rasped level with the others on the same jaw. Your vet should keep an eye on it.

Q. My mare is just recovering from an illness, and the vet has told me that I can now start turning her out again. How should I go about getting her used to this – I don't want her to injure herself tearing around the first time she goes out?

A. It is best to make sure that when you first turn her out she is hungry, so that she is likely to settle down more quickly to grazing. If possible, and if you think it will be beneficial to her, try and provide a quiet companion who will help her to settle. It is advisable to turn her out in a small paddock to start with, as this will discourage her from galloping around quite so madly – particularly if you are able to find somewhere to put her where she will be well away from other horses (other than her companion) whose presence could cause her to get over-excited. When you let her go, turn her head to the gate, so that she is unable to kick out at you the moment you release her. Leave the gate slightly ajar so that you are able to slip behind it quickly. Letting go is easiest managed if you leave the head-collar on, and loop a long lead rope through it, rather than clipping it on. All you have to do then is simply slip the rope.
If you are very worried about the possibility of her injuring herself, have a chat with your vet, who may advise giving her a mild sedative just beforehand. Do not leave her out for too long at first, but gradually build up the length of time she is out, as the change in her diet once she is grazing again could upset her stomach if the changeover is too sudden.

Q. My horse is plagued by flies in the summer months – is there a really effective repellent I can use for him?

A. Flies seem to be particularly attracted to dirty and sweating horses, and you may well find that regular bathing will help to lessen his attraction to them, particularly if you shampoo him with a product which has a mild antiseptic included in it. If you are unable to bath him properly after riding, a quick wash down with water and a sponge will certainly help. When flies are at their worst, your horse is unlikely to settle down to grazing, so you could also try stabling during the daytime; put up some fly papers to make it a real haven from them. When he does go out, or if you are unable to stable him, it is kindest if he has some shelter and the companionship of another pony or horse,

Fig. 39. Horses standing in the shade, nose to tail.

as they will be able to stand nose to tail and provide a mutual fly swatting service.

Try to avoid pulling tails or forelocks, and allow the tail to

Fig. 40. A fitted fly fringe.

grow to a reasonable length. If the forelock is on the sparse side, you could also buy a fly fringe or mask, which attaches to the headcollar. Many effective repellents and flybands are available from saddlers, but you will also find that oil of citronella (from the chemists) or even malt vinegar works well if your normal supplies of repellent run short. Feeding two chopped cloves of garlic in the short feed also seems to help lessen fly worry.

Q. Just recently my TB cross mare's coat has started to grow through lighter in the area where her saddle patch is. Her saddle fits her well – the saddler has been along and checked its fit. I was planning to show her this summer, but she looks rather odd. Is there any reason for this, or anything I can do to prevent it from getting worse?

A. This discolouration seems to happen quite frequently in horses with TB blood. Other than making sure the saddle fits correctly, there is not a great deal you can do about it, except to massage the saddle area after removing the saddle to ensure the return of normal blood circulation. As far as showing is concerned, it is possible to obtain different shades of hair dye which you could use to disguise the saddle patch. Try a small test area first, to check match of colour and that there are no skin reactions.

Q. My horse had a sore back last year, and the area which was rubbed has now healed up nicely. However, the hairs are now growing through white – will these turn back to brown eventually?

A. You should of course, try to prevent the rubbing from happening again, and check and correct the saddle, roller, or whatever the object was that caused the injury. It was obviously serious enough to damage the pigmentation cells, and now that the hairs have grown through white, they are there to stay.

Q. My pony has got broken wind. What can I do to keep him as comfortable as possible?

A. Any horse or pony with a cough or respiratory problem needs a good system of stable management. His environment needs to be kept as dust free as possible, so that the condition is not aggravated. The top doors of stables should never be closed, but left open so that the area is well ventilated, and he should be turned out to grass as much as possible, where he will be in the fresh air. When mucking out, the animal should be turned out, or transferred to another stable, and any dust left to settle before putting him back. Straw is not the ideal bedding, as it not only can be dusty, but is frequently eaten, distending the stomach which presses on the lungs. A substitute should be found; peat or shredded paper are ideal, or very clean woodshavings. These can be dampened down slightly by sprinkling the bed with diluted disinfectant. This will keep dust to a minimum, and also prevent any harmful, nibbling due to its unpleasant taste. Hay should be soaked for twenty four hours, or alternatively Horsehage or one of the other brands of dust and spore-free hay should be fed. All feeds should be dampened, and a cough mixture given to help soothe the throat if a cough is present. Grooming is best done out of doors, with the animal's head facing into the wind. Generally speaking, the fitter you can keep the pony, the better able to cope it will be; your vet will be able to advise you as to a limited exercise routine. Any horse or pony which is coughing (other than simply blowing its nose on the start of exercise) should not, however, be worked. The vet should be consulted at once.

Q. My horse's feet are very smelly, and there is a small amount of greasy, black coloured discharge, which is coming from the frog area. He is not lame – is this a normal condition?

A.   The condition described is 'Thrush' and if neglected could eventually lead to lameness. It arises through standing in wet, dirty, or muddy conditions, and through the feet not being picked out regularly enough. Keep stable bedding as clean as possible, skipped out frequently if your horse spends much time standing in, and with plenty of fresh clean bedding put down each day. Pick the feet out at least twice a day. Fill the toe of an old sock with garden lime, tie a knot in the end to stop everything coming out, and lightly tap the foot with it after picking out. A light dusting of lime will be left on the frog and sole, which will help to keep it dry and be slightly antiseptic. As the thrush is not yet too serious, and does not sound in need of poulticing, scrub the feet thoroughly after picking them out, tub each one in turn (see page 110), then dry and lime sock afterwards.

Q. A friend's horse had colic recently, and nearly died from it. What should I do if my horse gets an attack? And what are the first symptoms?

A. The symptoms vary considerably, depending on the type and cause of colic; the horse will generally appear distressed and uncomfortable. If stabled, the bedding may show signs of rolling, or the horse's restlessness. The top lip may be frequently curled back; it may kick at its stomach, or turn to look at it. It may just stand looking dejected, or in violent cases it will lie down and roll. It may be sweating, off its feed, have a tight, staring coat, and be straining to pass urine or droppings, but without success. Small, mucous covered droppings may be visible in the bed, or alternatively, the animal may be suffering from diarrhoea.

If it is a blockage type colic, there will be little or no bowel movement if you place your ear to the flanks; it is not a bad idea to be familiar with the normal rumbling which can be heard. If it is an enteritis type colic, there will on the other hand be an excessive amount of noise, and weight will quickly be lost; the horse quickly becoming visibly thinner. The horse may also rinse its mouth frequently with water, but without actually taking a drink.

On recognising any of these symptoms, and suspecting colic, you should ring your vet immediately, describing the behaviour, and how long it has been going on for. Whilst you are waiting for him to arrive, try to make the horse as comfortable as possible, although should the symptoms be violent, you should take care of your own safety too. Put him in a large airy stable with plenty of bedding which has been well banked up around the walls. If it is cold, put on stable bandages, and a rug with a sweat sheet beneath in case he begins to sweat. Do not fasten the roller, but leave the front straps undone, so that he is more comfortable; should the rugs slip, he will not become entangled in them, they will simply drop free. Leave a headcollar on in case you need to catch hold of him quickly. Allow him to lie down if he is happier like that, but do not allow him to roll; if he does try this, either get him back on his feet again, or sit on his head to keep him still so that he does not injure himself internally in his struggles.

Q. I am getting a medicine cabinet together for my horse; what should I stock it with?

A. If you are at all worried about your horse's health at any time, you should call the vet out straightaway, rather than meddling and perhaps making the situation worse. However, it doesn't hurt to have a few first aid things around, so that in

the event of an emergency, you are at least able to cope until
qualified assistance arrives. If your horse looks a little off colour,
it will also enable you to check up on him, and deal with minor
cuts. Keep all the things together; old drugs should be discarded
rather than saved once they have served their purpose, and the
entire box should be kept well out of the reach of animals or
young children. The following items should be included – more
can always be added at a future date if desired.

Thermometer	Epsom salts
Cotton wool	Table salt
Gamgee	Scissors
Stable bandages x 4	Insulating tape
Crepe bandages x 2	Record book
Glucose	Elasticated support bandages x 4
Vaseline	Poultices (Kaolin and Animalintex)
Antiseptic cream	Antibiotic spray

*Q. How should I deal with simple cuts, and which ones should
I call the vet to treat?*

A.   The first thing you must do if your horse cuts himself is
to assess the seriousness of the injury, and whether it is likely
to need more experienced help and treatment. These instances
are:
If a cut looks as though it will need stitching.
If a vein or artery has been nicked or severed.
If a joint has been damaged (other than minor cuts).
If a bone is broken, or suspected to be.
If an anti-tetanus booster is required.
Or any occasion when you feel that you are unable to treat an
injury competently yourself.
    If a vein or artery has been damaged, you should try to arrest
the bleeding until the vet comes. In the case of arterial bleeding
(identified by its bright red colour, which spurts since it is still
under the pumping influence of the heart) you should press a
clean pad firmly over the area and apply digital pressure. Vei-
nous bleeding (maroon in colour and a steady flow) is best
treated by running a hosepipe at low pressure over the injury
to constrict the blood vessels, so lessening the amount of blood
lost. If a bone is broken, then no pressure should be applied
other than a low pressure hosepipe if necessary to stop bleeding,
and the animal should not be moved. The types of cuts which
you are most likely to encounter are:

Punctures – caused by a pointed object such as a thorn or nail. These can be quite dangerous since the wound is often deeper than at first suspected, and sometimes escapes notice altogether. If the object is still embedded, it should be carefully removed, noting the depth and angle to which it has penetrated, and the wound should then be poulticed to remove any possible source of infection.

Abrasions – these are grazes, often occurring as a result of jumping solid fences, or falling on the roads. The area should be cleaned as thoroughly as possible, and then poulticed, as it is likely that dirt will have become worked in.

Incisions – clean cuts may be caused by broken glass. Unless they are very deep, bleeding is usually minimal, and provided they are properly cleaned and treated regularly with an antiseptic cream, are unlikely to cause very much trouble.

Contusions – this is a bruise, where the skin is not broken, but as a direct result of a blow – possibly a kick from another horse or pony – tissues and blood vessels have become broken, giving rise to a warm, tender swelling. Alternate hot and cold poulticing or fomentations are usually the best way of repairing the damage and reducing the swelling.

Lacerations – tear wounds can be quite serious, many arising because of poor maintenance of barbed wire fencing. They may also occur when a bone shatters, and splinters are forced outwards from within, breaking through the skin. There is often quite a bit of bleeding, since a large number of blood vessels have been damaged. The injury should be treated carefully, hosing with a low pressure hose to clean it. If stitching is needed, the vet should be called promptly if the wound is to close up satisfactorily. If the cut is fairly minor, then treating with antiseptic cream after cleaning is usually quite adequate.

Overreach – this happens when the toe of a back foot catches the heel of a front foot, inflicting a cut. It may be overlooked at first, as a flap of skin may conceal the injury. The flap of dead skin should be cut off first of all, so that the area can be easily treated, and so that dirt does not become trapped beneath. After hosing it clean, it should then be poulticed, until clean. Afterwards a dry dressing can be used until the injury has healed over sufficiently to prevent dirt getting in.

The most effective way of cleaning a cut is to hose it, since this is less likely to work dirt in. If the injury is in an area where hosing may be difficult or impossible to manage, then a piece of cotton wool may be soaked in salty water and squeezed out over it. Disinfectants should not be used as they are likely to retard healing; salty water is a far better antiseptic wash. If the legs need to be hosed frequently in order to keep a cut clean, the heels should be vaselined to keep them from chapping or cracking.

The best way to clean a foot injury, such as a punctured sole, is by tubbing. The foot should be picked out and scrubbed to remove the worst of the dirt. The heels should be smeared with vaseline, and then the foot can be held above a shallow bowl to which clean hot water and a double handful of Epsom salts have been added. A little of the water should be ladled over the foot, accustoming the horse to the temperature, before gently lowering the foot into the bowl. It may be useful to have an assistant pick up the opposite leg in order to discourage fidgeting around during this process. From time to time as the water cools, the bowl should be topped up again with more hot water, but the level should never be allowed to rise above the coronary band, or else instead of being drawn out of the foot, dirt and infection will be drawn upwards. Tubbing should continue for about twenty minutes, after which the foot can be dried and poulticed. It should be tubbed again each time before poulticing.

Q.   I have just bought a pony which had an attack of laminitis two years ago. I am worried in case he gets it again; what should I do to try and prevent it?

A.   Laminitis is an acutely painful condition for any pony, and precautions should be taken to prevent its occurrence in animals most likely to be susceptible, and the recurrence in those that have been affected before. The condition itself is an inflammation of the sensitive laminae of the hoof – these are fine tissue-like structures which support the pedal bone and contain large amounts of blood. With the onset of laminitis, these laminae begin to break down, and if the situation is allowed to become very bad, the pedal bone may begin to drop downwards, until it penetrates the sole of the foot. By the time this stage has been reached, the animal is usually in considerable pain, and the kindest option is to have it put out of its misery. There are a number of causes; too much work on hard surfaces, following an attack of colic or after foaling, being given a cold drink when hot. It has most frequently come to be associated with native

Fig. 41. A laminitic pony – the typical stance with its weight on its heels.

ponies though, who are overweight, underexercised, and on too rich a diet. The symptoms are a reluctance to move around, lying down for unusually long periods of time, standing with the weight on the heels, a raised temperature, which may be accompanied by sweating, warm or hot feet. A swollen sheath or udder can sometimes give an early warning, since it is often symptomatic of an overfed animal which is not exercised sufficiently. The moment you notice any of these signs, particularly since your pony has suffered before, you should notify the vet.

Best of all, you should attempt to prevent the onset. Restrict the grazing, particularly during the Spring and Autumn flushes of grass. This may be done by either fencing off an area of the field, moving to a barer paddock, or stabling for part of the time. Do not allow the pony to become overweight, but try to keep him a little on the lean side. Exercise regularly, since this will also help to stop him from becoming overweight, and be sure to stick to the minimum necessary amount of hard feed for the work he is doing. He should be regularly shod every four to six weeks too, so that his heels do not become overlong, as this could lead to bad circulation back up the leg from the foot.

Q. My pony has started to rub his mane and tail a lot; is this just due to the fact that the weather is getting warmer and he is changing his coat?

A.   This could be due either to lice or to sweet-itch. Lice will be noticed during the Spring months, and look very much like small hay seeds. These can be got rid of by sprinkling a louse powder along the roots of the mane on both sides, along the spine, and on the tail. This should be repeated two weeks later. Check up on the last date of worming too, as worm infestation can cause irritation around the anus.

The other possibility is that it could signify the onset of sweet-itch. This is a form of non-contagious dermatitis which causes intense irritation; affected animals will often rub the areas along

Fig. 42. A sweet-itch-affected pony, with its rubbed mane and tail.

the crest, withers, and top of the dock until they are raw and bleeding. It is thought that the cause is an allergic reaction to certain biting midges, and it seems to be most common in the native breeds, cobs, and hunters. The condition will occur during the spring and summer months, often continuing well into the autumn if the weather is mild. No cure has yet been discovered, and treatment consists mainly of prevention as far as possible, and the use of drugs and lotions aimed at relieving the discomfort. As soon as the weather gets warmer, you should stable your pony during the daytime, only turning him out once it is dark – twilight and early morning especially are bad times for midges and to be avoided, but bright sunlight also seems to aggravate the situation. Being overweight does not help either, and feeding barley should be avoided. Fly repellents should be used, and a fly strip can be hung up in the stable. Bathing the affected areas frequently with cold water seems to ease matters, and calamine lotion, benzyl-benzoate, or one of the sweet-itch lotion brand-name products can be used to provide relief and stimulation of hair regrowth. You should also consult your vet, as he may be able to administer antihistamine or cortisone injections.

Q. When should I call the vet?

A.   At any time when your horse or pony appears to be unwell, and also for routine checkups. His teeth should be checked every six months, and he should be covered by a 'flu injection each year, and an anti tetanus injection every two years. If he is lame, has a cough, or shows any signs of worrying abnormal behaviour, you should also call the vet. When looking at a horse in good health, its general attitude should be one of alertness, and yet relaxation, and of general well-being, covered with plenty of flesh without actually being gross. It should stand and move comfortably, with no signs of lameness. Taking a closer look, the eyes should be bright, with no signs of discharge. The mucous membrances of both eyes, nostrils and gums, should be salmon pink in colour. A yellowish tinge indicates jaundice, red a fever, a bluish red tinge heart trouble, and pale membranes anaemia. There should be no discharge from the nostrils, other than perhaps a small amount of clear nasal gleate; if it increases in quantity, becomes thick, or discoloured, it indicates the presence of infection.

The appetite should be good, but normal; not eating voraciously, but neither picking at, or leaving, food. There should be no trouble in mastication. The limbs should all be free from unusual lumps and bumps. The coat should lie flat, with a healthy sheen on it; a tight, staring coat is an indication of ill health, and often accompanies worm infestation and malnutrition. The urine should be nearly colourless and free of offensive odour, whilst the droppings should be firm and rounded, just breaking slightly as they hit the ground. Small, hard droppings coated with mucous may indicate constipation and worms, whilst diarrhoea is often due to a digestive upset or gut irritation. The horse should not sweat (unless he has just been exercised hard). A hot sweat without such justification indicates pain, an elevated temperature, or a fever, whilst a cold sweat may break out if there is pain or mental disturbance.

The temperature in a healthy horse or pony should be approximately 100–101.5°F, although this may vary slightly from one individual to another, and according to the time of year, so it is important to know what is right for your own particular animal. The temperature may be taken by shaking down a veterinary thermometer, lubricating the bulb with a little liquid paraffin or vaseline, and then inserting it into the rectum for a minute and a half. It should be angled slightly so that it rests against the bowel wall, and not in the middle of a ball of faeces. Ask an assistant to hold the horse throughout, as some are not co-operative about the procedure. After use, disinfect the thermometer and put it away again ready for future use. A rise in temperature of two or three degrees above normal means that pain is present. If higher, that there is an infection. Respiration should be around 8 – 12 inhalations/exhalations per minute in a normal horse standing at rest. Stand slightly to the back and one side of the quarters in order to see the movement of the flanks quite clearly. Count each time that they either move inwards, or outwards. The pulse should be in the region of 35 – 40 per minute. It can be felt anywhere that an artery crosses a bone, but the easiest place is probably just beneath the jaw bone, in front of the cheek.

11

Shows

Q. How can I find out where local shows are being held?

A.   Each year the weekly magazine 'Horse and Hound' publishes a show directory which provides a guide as to dates and whereabouts of show fixtures, generally spread over two issues. If you miss these, a weekly guide is published in the same magazine for show dates for the forthcoming week. Most horsy magazines also publish adverts for shows, whilst smaller, more local events are often publicised in the local press. It is always worth enquiring at local saddlers, riding schools and livery yards, and feed merchants, as show secretaries often distribute schedules for events to such places. If you write to your local Riding and Saddle Club secretaries, you should also be able to obtain a programme of events scheduled for the season ahead.

Q. I'd like to do some cross country competitions with my youngster, but I don't really think he is quite ready for the pressure of a competition proper. How can I give him some experience though, without actually having to enter a class?

A.   Many cross country competitions run a clear round section either at the beginning or end of the day, usually over smaller obstacles. This would give you both the opportunity of gaining experience under show conditions, but when it is a little quieter, and without being thrown out if you get a couple of stops at a tricky fence. A number of yards possessing cross country facilities hold schooling days, or will hire the course out for a small fee, which is another alternative for you to consider. This would also give you more opportunity of trying different approaches to different fences. The charges can often be reduced if you hire the course with a group of friends, and this would also give you the advantage of having other horses around to give you a lead if you got into difficulties.

Fig. 43. A horse jumping a cross country fence (being watched by another rider).

Q.   Should I trim up my native pony to show in Mountain and Moorland classes? I always thought they were supposed to be left entirely alone, but a friend has told me that my pony would look much better tidied up.

A.   There is a difference between 'trimming up' and 'tidying up'. Although you should leave the mane, tail, and feathers untrimmed, there is no doubt that a little bit of judicious tidying up will greatly improve the appearance. Trim the whiskers off around the muzzle and jawline, also the edge of the ears. The tail, although left long, can be trimmed squarely at the end. Some breed classes are more tolerant than others of the degree of trimming up than others; in New Forest classes for example, you can get away with a pulled mane and tail, whilst to do such a thing to a Welsh Cob or Fell would be very much frowned upon. It is never a waste of time visiting a few shows as a spectator rather than a competitor to see what is expected in each of the different breed classes – or you could contact the Secretary of the breed society.

Q.   I am taking my young son and his pony in a leading rein class at a local show shortly. Should the lead rein be clipped to the bit or the noseband?

A.   The lead rein should be clipped to the noseband, and the pony seen to be moving freely forward and in response to his rider, rather than having to be restrained or dragged along by the person leading.

Fig. 44.
(a) The correct way to attach a lead rein in lead rein classes.
(b) A pony in a lead rein class.

Q. My horse has a great deal of ability showjumping, and I would now like to enter him for some affiliated shows – how do I set about this?

A. You will need to be a member of the BSJA (British Showjumping Association), and your horse will also need to be registered with them. Membership will entitle you to receive a quarterly newsletter containing news and show dates, plus other discounts. Further information can be obtained, (see page 151).

Q. I would like to take up showjumping more seriously, but am finding it very expensive by the time I have paid for travelling and entry fees. How should I set about finding a sponsor so that I can carry on?

A. Nowadays, when it is becoming increasingly expensive to keep a horse, let alone to compete with it on a regular basis, everybody is on the lookout for a sponsor. When approaching a possible sponsor, you should first remember to aim at sponsorship suitable to the level of competition you intend to do. If you are going to be riding at Riding Club shows, your best bet is to approach small local firms rather than large nationwide ones. There is no point in tackling a large company unless you have a good track record riding in affiliated competition, as a big company will be more interested in nationwide publicity. Often, for a competitor who does not command the sort of following and publicity which top international riders can muster, it is more successful to approach a small local company and compete in shows in the area.

To have any success in finding a sponsor, you will have to do some footwork first. Rather than just writing and hoping for a favourable reply to your suggestions, it is often best to make an appointment and call in for a personal visit. Do not exclude any firm as being too small – you could check out the possibility of assistance from grocery shops, small firms which trade in your area, perhaps even a pub. At the interview you will need to try and make the right sort of impression, and sound very confident of your abilities. If you do not feel able to manage this, then it might be a good idea to get a friend to make the initial moves on your behalf. If someone is interested in you as a good potential proposition for publicity, they will almost certainly want to meet you first before committing themselves though, so it is not something which can be put off forever. You will need to show some kind of form – it is no good simply pulling out a horse and telling your sponsor how good it is going to be. It must already have demonstrated ability and success. A horse which refuses the first fence in the novice is not going to leave a lasting impression on anybody's mind. It will help if you can produce a record of your achievements, preferably with the horse which you would like sponsored, backed up if possible with a few good photographs of the two of you in action at a show. Try and be fairly smart when meeting your sponsor – first impressions are often lasting ones, and if you are dressed like a tramp, he may well change his mind. You must ooze confidence, and be businesslike in your manner; work out all the facts and figures in advance so that you have all the information he will require at your fingertips, and will not be seen to be dithering. Know what kind of deal you are after. Prepare a list of future shows, their dates, venues, and how many classes you will enter at each. Decide on what expenses you are likely to incur, and what percentage you would ideally like your sponsor to cover. Don't be greedy, as a small firm won't be able to afford the expense – you have to compete favourably with the sort of publicity which can be gained from placing an advert in the local newspaper. It is better to have a little help than none at all, and it will prove that you are sufficiently sure of your capabilities if you are willing to put some of your own cash.

Travelling expenses are pretty hefty, so it might be best to just settle for these initially. You are unlikely to find a local company which is willing to support your horse totally. Later on, when you have proved yourself, you may find them willing to invest more money in you, or you will be able to find a larger company which can afford more. Of course, sponsorship is a two-way arrangement; you will hope to benefit from it, but so does your sponsor. Point out that the cost of your travelling, for example, works out at rather less than the price of a boxed advert in the local paper; and remind him of the wide range of people you will be seen by. It is not solely horsy people who go to shows, but they are frequently a family outing as well. You will have to be prepared to wear the company or shop's logo or name on your rugs, and will have to come to some agreement about who keeps the trophies and rosettes – it is usually only fair that the sponsor keeps them. Come to some agreement about any prize money; whether you will retain it or divide it – it is best to have something in writing about these points to avoid dispute in the future.

If you manage to gain sponsorship, you will also have to make the effort to be polite, cheerful, and helpful to everyone you speak to, so that you promote your sponsors' image, rather than destroy it. You will in effect be on show as a sort of spokesman on his behalf. At all times both you and your horse will have to display immaculate appearance and turnout, and prove to be a good sportsman. Losing your temper is not a good thing to happen at the best of times, and is even less so when in the eye of the public and a sponsor.

Q. I would like to take my four year old to some shows. She has quite an excitable nature though – how can I make her first shows as quiet an introduction as possible?

A. Preparation plays a large part in making first shows trouble free. If you are planning on travelling her in a lorry or trailer, make sure that she is familiar with everything, from being bandaged up to actually travelling. The more she feels at home the better – a battle in the middle of a showground will unsettle her. Work her occasionally with other horses, so that she is less distracted by them. On the day of the show, try to leave early; if you are hacking there, it will help to take the edge off and settle her down. If travelling in a lorry or trailer, give her some exercise before setting off. Select quiet classes to start with, such as Best Condition and Best Turnout, where she will only be required to walk around. Such classes are also normally the first ones on the schedule, which will suit your purposes, as the showground is unlikely to be too busy.

If you wish to jump her, stick to Clear Round classes until you are sure that she is going to take everything calmly and in her stride. Give her the chance to relax and become used to the different atmosphere, whatever the type of class you are going to enter for, so that she has the chance to have a good look around, and then settle down and concentrate on her work. When in a showing class, try not to get jammed in between horses, which can be an upsetting experience for a youngster. Above all, remember that you are out to start her competitive career off on the right foot, not to upset her completely. If you arrive and find that she is very uptight, just hack her quietly around for a little, and if things don't improve, take her home again without actually going in the ring. Another day she will be better behaved for having been introduced to shows quietly and carefully. Consider other people's horses besides yours; if your mare causes a riot, nobody will be very happy at the end of the day!

Q. I want to enter some gymkhana classes with my new pony, but I am not sure what you have to do for each one. What is involved? Is there any special schooling needed? My mum said she would like to try some too (she exercises my pony to keep him fit whilst I am at school). Is she too old?

A. It would be a good idea to go to a gymkhana just to watch, as you can pick up a lot of tips by watching more experienced riders, as well as learning about the races. It is something that your mother can have a go at too, since there are usually different heats for different age groups, including one for adults. Since the races can be pretty tiring though, it would be best if you rode in different races rather than the same ones. Since your mother is also able to exercise your pony, she should also be able to keep him pretty fit – you will be surprised just how much energy he will need. Do not forget your own fitness though – try skipping, running, cycling, or swimming so that you do not let him down. You can also practise plenty of dismounted things such as running in a sack for the sack race (the knack is to stick a toe in each corner of the sack and run, rather than hop!). Teach your pony to lead freely in hand, and try to ensure that he is as supple and obedient as possible. Practise standing starts, vaulting on and off, and set out rows of cones or oil drums to practise bending and turning around. There are quite a few different gymkhana games, and the rules seem to vary slightly from one show to another. However, the basics of each game are laid down in a book entitled 'Mounted Games and Gymkhanas' published by the Pony Club. Most people are quite happy to help if you are in any confusion – and do watch the heat before you!

Q. I would like to be better at gymkhana classes. The trouble is that I can't vault on, so I lose a lot of time fiddling about with my stirrups. How can I get better at this – or should I just train my pony to kneel down for me instead?!

A. This is definitely something which needs to be practised at home, rather than hoping that somehow you will manage once in the ring. Instead of trying to heave yourself on as though trying to climb a brick wall, you will find it easier if you take a large handful of mane in your left hand, stand as you would when mounting normally, then really swing your right leg over your pony's back, jumping off your left foot at the same time.

Fig. 45. Vaulting onto a pony.

If you have a biggish pony, it is easiest to get the knack by borrowing a friend's smaller pony to start with. Then gradually work up to a bigger pony, and start practising vaulting on, not just in halt, but trot and canter too.

Q.   What sort of show should I give in a showing class? If my pony canters on the wrong leg should I stop and start again, or just carry on?

A.   Keep your show short and simple – do not attempt anything you are not sure of achieving. Whilst waiting for your turn, plan where you are going to ride your individual show, trying to stick to the places where the ground is reasonably level, not too cut up, and where the judge has a good view of you. You may be specifically asked to do something, otherwise when it is your turn, just walk forward out of the line and halt in front of the judge so that he/she has a good view of your pony. Then walk on, trot a circle on each rein, and canter a figure of eight, trotting in the centre to change legs. If you get the wrong canter lead, trot and ask again. If asked to gallop, choose a sensible place to do it, steadying for any corners, and taking care not to mow anybody down! Practise your show at home, so that you both know it off by heart, and things are less likely to go wrong. To finish, walk back to the judge again, halt and rein back if you are able, and then rejoin the line.

Q.   What sort of clothes do I need to wear for showing classes?

A.   Unless you are competing at a very large show, hacking dress is usually fine for most classes, and within the reach of most people's finances. This consists of a hacking jacket, shirt, tie, beige, cream or lemon (never white) jodhpurs, yellow string gloves, long boots for an adult and jodhpur boots for a child. A hunting cap or bowler should be worn by ladies whilst men should always wear a bowler – although if it proves to be too expensive, a hunting cap should be fine for most local shows. Some classes, such as Best Turnout do require hunting dress (unless hacking turnout is specified). This consists of a black jacket, hunting shirt and hunting tie, white or yellow breeches, long boots, spurs, gloves, bowler and a hunt whip. There are no real rules about what to wear if you are showing in hand; however it should be practical and workmanlike. A sensible skirt, or corduroy trousers or similar, plus a jacket, sturdy shoes, and a bowler are fine, or else your riding clothes if you have

Fig. 46. Hacking and hunting dress.

just been riding. A showing cane should be carried in classes where hacking dress is worn, and also when competing in In Hand classes. Do pay attention to turnout; make sure there are no creases in clothes, that they are clean, and correctly worn. Unless it is very short, hair should be tied back or netted, and men should remember to shave! There are many excellent books on showing, and it is worth reading a few of these, and attending a few shows to watch, to pick up further tips and hints on correct turnout.

12

Travelling

Q. I need to hire a lorry or trailer to take my pony to a show in, as it is too far to hack. Where can I hire one from?

A. It is worth asking around locally, as someone near you may be going to the same show and have room in their trailer or lorry for an extra passenger if you chip in some money to help pay for part of the petrol or diesel used. Otherwise, ask at local riding schools, livery yards, or saddlers as to a reputable horse transporter in your area – or else look in Yellow Pages.

Q. Which side of my double trailer should I travel my horse on – right or left? Or should I take out the central partition altogether?

A. You should travel your horse on the right (off) side of the trailer, as this will help to compensate the camber of the road, and so give a steadier and more comfortable ride. The same applies when travelling two animals of different weights; place the heavier one on the off side. When travelling a single horse in a trailer (or vehicle) which is designed to carry two or more animals of that size, then you should put the partition up to prevent the horse from being thrown about, and to encourage it to stand still.

Q. I am travelling my horse to a show soon – he is supposed to be good to load and so on, so does he still need to wear protective clothing? And what sort?

A. If you have never travelled your horse before, it could be a wise idea to try a dummy run before the day of the show, just to check that he really is going to behave. If he is likely to prove awkward, then at least you will know that you must leave some extra time on the morning if you are to arrive on time for your classes. You should also practise dressing him up in his travelling gear in case he has never worn any before. This

Fig. 47. A horse dressed for travelling.

can be quite a frightening experience for youngsters especially if they have never had much handling. What you choose by way of protective clothing to guard him from knocks and bumps during the journey depends upon the weather, your expertise and personal preferences. If it is cold and the horse is clipped, then he should wear a warm stable or day rug, with a sweat sheet beneath in case he starts to sweat up in excitement. During the summer, a light cotton or linen summer sheet will help to keep draughts off his back without overheating him; but take the precaution of putting a sweat sheet beneath the sheet anyway.

On his legs you should put travelling bandages, with squares of gamgee, fybagee or cotton pads beneath so that he is well padded against accidental bumps. It is important to bandage fairly low, as the lower regions of the legs are most likely to get hurt. Bandages will also keep his legs clean on the way to a show – if he has white socks, chalk them before bandaging. If you are not very proficient at bandaging, and find them too fiddly, or your horse tends to fidget, you could put travelling boots on as an alternative. These are usually very well lined, and take only a few minutes to put on or take off, and there is no danger of accidentally injuring the horse by bandaging wrongly. The knees and hocks can be protected by knee and hock boots, and if you are concerned that he may tread on himself, then put overreach boots on all round. These are easiest to put on and remove if they are the split variety, fastened by velcro tapes. A poll guard can be put on in case he lifts his head abruptly and bangs it – if you do not wish to buy one, it is easy enough to buy a thick strip of foam rubber quite cheaply, and fasten it to the headpiece of the headcollar. Finally, a tail bandage should be put on to prevent the hairs of the tail from becoming broken. If the tail bandage has a tendency to slip downwards, you could use a tail guard made of rugging or leather in addition to, or instead of, the tail bandage.

Q.   My horse's problem is not in being loaded, or when actually travelling – he is very well behaved and never any bother about this. But when he is unloaded, he shoots out of the trailer in reverse, coming out very fast. How can I get him to take things more steadily, before he hurts himself?

A.   Firstly, do make sure that he has plenty of protective boots or bandages in case the worst happens. Practise unloading him at home, not just when you go to shows, when the atmosphere is bound to make him more tense. Check that the breeching

Fig. 48. A broom is held ready to push against the quarters of a horse which rushes out when being unloaded.

strap is strong so that you have plenty of time to lower the ramp – you do not want him to come charging out before you are quite ready. The ramp itself should have struts nailed across its breadth to give more grip; you could put some coconut matting or rubber grip mats down too so that he does not slip. Put a bridle on him, which will give you a bit more control, and do not forget the power of the human voice to soothe and calm any fears that he might have. Position an assistant at the bottom of the ramp, with another ready to undo the breeching strap on your command. The first assistant should be ready with a yard broom, and as the breeching strap is undone, can gently rest the bristles against the quarters – this provides some incentive not to rush out. If possible, and they are not already present, get some tail gates fitted, as these will keep him straight and stop him from slipping over the edge of the ramp. You might also try him in a front unload trailer some time, as he may be less inclined to try and stampede out.

Q.   My horse is good whilst travelling – except when the trailer is standing still, at traffic lights, junctions and so on, when she always starts kicking. If she doesn't hurt herself first, I am worried that she will damage the trailer.

A.   The only answer in this case is to hobble her once she is loaded up. Make sure that they are well lined with sheepskin or gamgee so that they do not chafe, and remember to take them off again before trying to unload!

Q.   My pony is really naughty about being loaded. What are the best ways of getting him to behave? Sometimes it takes hours to get him into the trailer, which means that we miss classes at shows.

A.   A horse or pony which is difficult to load can be very irritating, and it is worth spending some time at home teaching him to be more co-operative, rather than having a fight each time that you want to load him up and go somewhere. If he tends to back off, and throw his head around, he may well have had a bad experience in the past which he still remembers. If he is young, he may just be nervous. Both types need coaxing, although this needs to be combined with a degree of firmness, since if he once learns his own strength, he will never forget or be slow to take advantage of it.

Start off by leading him forward towards the ramp of the

trailer, with a bridle on to give you more control. Make sure that the trailer itself is parked on level ground, with chocks beneath the ramp if necessary to prevent it from wobbling when weight is placed on it. The more solid it looks and feels, the more confident he is likely to be about going in. Put the stands down if there are any, leave the towing vehicle in gear, and engage the trailer handbrake. If possible, park it alongside a wall or fence so that there is one less obvious escape route. The interior should be bedded down with straw to give both grip and to damp the noise a little – rubber grip matting will help to do the same. A haynet can be tied up securely and in full view, and the central partition if there is one, can be moved across to make more room. If it is a front unload trailer, the front ramp can be lowered to make it all look less 'trappy' and confined.

Walk forwards towards the ramp, remaining between the pony's eye and shoulder; if you try and drag him along, then he is more likely to pull back in resistance than to give in and follow. If he hesitates, offer a tempting feed in a bucket, and try enticing him in. If he does go in, then the feed can be offered as a reward, so that he comes to associate being loaded as a pleasurable event. If he still proves obstinate, and is not likely to kick out, you could get your assistant to try moving his feet one by one up the ramp. Alternatively a lunge rein can be fastened to one side of the trailer, looped around the quarters above the hocks, and pulled taut at the opposite side by your assistant, who should wear gloves so that his/her hands do not become sore. Some horses will immediately give in when they feel something pushing around their quarters, whilst others may need a good tug on the lunge rein before walking in. Should he begin to panic, and reverse rapidly, try and kick out, or rear, you should stop at once, as he is more likely to injure himself than go in. You may have to resort to the more lengthy process of bribing him with titbits again.

Sometimes thirst will overcome any fears; leave him without water for 12 hours and then offer him a bucket of water. Allow a short drink if he walks in as a reward.

Some horses and ponies are just naughty about loading, and in such cases, a quick reminder is all that is needed. The easiest approach is to have your assistant hold a yard broom behind the quarters, and to give him a couple of shoves with it. This makes him uncomfortable enough to think twice about digging his heels in, and he will be unable to kick out at the assistant

Fig. 49. Holding a lunge rein around the quarters of a pony, with the trailer parked against a wall.

due to the length of the broom handle. Once in, fasten the breeching strap, reward with a titbit and plenty of praise, and repeat the procedure several times each day until he walks in without any hesitation. If you feed him each day whilst he is loaded, he will soon come to look forward to going in. Once he has started to behave rather better, you may want to take him on some short trips. Since there is often a reason for being bad about loading, make sure that it is not due to being given a bad ride by the driver. With time and patience he should get better – but however awkward he may be, do not be tempted to try and ride him in, as this could be extremely dangerous should he try and rear with you on top.

Q.   I am moving house shortly, and will be travelling my horse up to my new home, which is about 300 miles away. Should I stop for a break on the way? If so, should I get my horse out and allow him to stretch his legs?

A.   Use your common sense. The types of road you will be travelling along will make a difference to the amount of time the journey takes, and the degree of stress it will place on the horse. Motorways make for more comfortable and direct driving than twisty, winding roads. Stop every two hours and check on your horse to make sure that he is comfortable, and to offer him a drink of water. He can have a haynet to nibble at, but avoid giving him a concentrate feed whilst in transit. If you really have to, then divide his normal ration into smaller portions which can be fed little and often, otherwise travel colic can arise. Make sure that there is plenty of bedding on the floor; although rubber matting provides good grip, and seems to absorb a certain amount of vibration, your horse may be reluctant to stale without a proper bed. Keep an eye on him and see how he is coping with the journey; should he not stale, and appear uncomfortable because of this, you could break the journey somewhere suitable and unload him so that he has the opportunity to relieve himself.

Q.   *I am about to buy a trailer, but have never actually towed one before. Are there any tips which would help me?*

A.   If you are unused to towing, here are some hints. Firstly, although the speed limit for trailers being towed is 50 mph, this is a *maximum* speed rather than the recommended one. If you are to give your horse a comfortable ride, everything must be in comparatively slow motion. Before loading him up for the first time, you would be well advised to practise driving with the trailer empty until you are accustomed to it – practise on the roads, and work at learning to manoeuvre it competently in a large field. To help you when manoeuvring, you will find it helpful to have proper wing mirrors – if those on your towing vehicle are inadequate or missing, you can purchase these from a caravan accessory shop. Adjust them so that you can see both the trailer mudguards and the road behind you.

Only once you feel confident in your abilities should you risk taking your horse out as a passenger – bad driving will quickly turn him into a poor traveller or bad loader. Anticipate hazards well in advance – avoid driving over cats' eyes, and choose good roads when possible, even if it will take a little longer to reach your destination than a short cut over badly made, hilly and twisty lanes. Start braking earlier at junctions, and take corners slower and slightly wider, giving plenty of room to any vehicles you overtake. Make sure that the trailer is quite safe before setting off anywhere. The tyres should be identical (i.e. cross-ply or radial, not a mixture on the same axis) with a minimum 1·6mm tread depth and with the correct pressure. The lights should all function properly, and any reflectors required all present and in place; do not forget to fix a number plate the same as the towing vehicle's. Make sure that when hitched up the trailer rides level, or very slightly nose downwards. If it points upwards it may cause snaking, whilst if it points downwards excessively there will be a vagueness about the steering.

Q. How often should I have my trailer serviced?

A. You should have it serviced every six months; the brakes and all moving parts must be checked, and the towball and towbar may also need some attention as they have to undergo quite a lot of stress. Do get it done by someone who knows what they are doing though – a botched up job could mean a risk to your horse.

Q. I am going to buy a trailer shortly, but am unsure as to what would be best.

A. This depends upon the size of the animal(s) you wish to tow, and the type of vehicle you intend to tow with. Do not tow up to the Legal Maximum Weight limit, but rather allow yourself to be guided by the recommended trailer towing weights. Each manufacturer publishes a weight, taking into account the size of the engine, the car's overall length, weight, gearing and suspension, and you should follow these. Otherwise, by attempting to tow too much, you could not only be liable to prosecution if your load is considered unsafe, but it will be difficult to control in bad or emergency conditions if the towing vehicle is not powerful and heavy enough. Most manufacturers or dealers will be only too happy to discuss your requirements, and to suggest a suitable trailer for your purposes.

Q. I am thinking of buying a secondhand trailer; what sort of things should I look out for?

A. There are quite a few checks which should be carried out for condition, safety and roadworthiness. The floor must be sound, not rotted, and the chassis in good condition. The shock absorbers ought to be properly working on the hitch, the brakes working and so forth. As when buying a secondhand car, it is best if you can take someone with you who is at least mechanically minded, and knows a little about trailers.

13

Riding Schools and Training

Q. I should like to learn to ride, but am rather nervous, and not sure how to go about finding a good riding school. I am worried that I might also be too old to learn.

A.   Being nervous is nothing to be ashamed of; what is important is that you find a school where you feel relaxed and at ease, so that any fears you may have will be put at rest. Personal

Fig. 50. A group lesson.

recommendations are best, but if you do not have any friends who ride, look in Yellow Pages to find out where your local riding schools are, and choose one which is either BHS or ABRS approved. The next step is to go along to have a look around before you book a lesson. When you arrive, take in your surroundings; they needn't be palatial, but they should at least be clean and tidy. The horses should all look healthy and happy, and any staff should also be tidy and workmanlike, and adding an air of efficiency to the place.

Go over to the office and introduce yourself, explaining that you are interested in learning to ride; ask if they have any suitable groups for beginners, and when they are held. To start with, they will probably recommend that you have a few lessons on your own, so that you have some basic control before joining other riders. The attitude of the staff and instructors should be cheerful, friendly, and informative (try and watch a lesson if possible) but if you feel that this yard is not quite your scene, do not be put off, try another. For your first lessons, wear a sensible pair of trousers which are not too tight, plus some reasonably flat shoes. The sole should be smooth, not ridged, with a small, well defined heel of about ½″ in height – sandals, trainers, wellington boots and wedge heels are not safe. The riding school should be able to lend you a hat for your first few lessons, then if you decide that you are enjoying the sport, you could then buy your own, plus some jodhpurs and riding boots. As far as age is concerned, you should not worry – provided you take things steadily and are in reasonable health, you should derive as much enjoyment as someone far younger, although you may find yourself perhaps feeling a little stiffer!

Q. I'd like to hire a horse or a pony so that I can go out for rides with my friend and her horse. Would a riding school do this?

A.   It is highly unlikely that a riding school – or any other sort of yard would allow you to hire a horse or pony without any escort or supervision from one of their staff. A private hire is likely to cost you a great deal more than if you were to join a group of other people, since a member of staff will have to be spared for just one person. You may find this irritating, but remember that it is not in their interest to allow a relatively unknown quantity to take a valuable animal out unaccompanied – it could end up injured, or too tired to be used on any lessons for a day or so. The chances are that their insurance policy does not extend to hire of horses except to accompanied clients, and this cover is after all, for the rider's benefit as much as the school's. However, should you wish to enter shows, some schools do take carefully supervised groups to local events, or hold their own competitions, which would at least give you the opportunity to compete occasionally.

Q.   I'd like to specialise more on dressage; the riding school I ride at seems to be geared towards jumping all the time. How can I go about learning more?

A.   Have a chat with your instructor. If you are in a group lesson, most people usually want to jump rather than concentrate solely on flatwork, so it is often a case of doing a little of everything in order to try and keep the majority happy. Unfortunately, this means that you are unable to progress quite as quickly towards your own particular goal. You might find that the occasional private lesson would be of benefit to you, since although it will cost more, the instruction is more concentrated and the lesson can be structured towards doing the things you are especially interested in. Alternatively, ask if there is a different group you can join, which does less jumping. Explain your ambitions; most instructors are only too happy to accommodate, but they are not mind readers and will not know unless you tell them! Should this prove impossible to manage, then you could always change to a different riding school. If you consult the BHS publication 'Where to Ride' you will find listed therein the facilities, level of instruction, and any specialised tuition available at each yard, so that you can pick one out which sounds right for you.

Q.   I'm not very good at riding, and I'd like to get more experience, also at stable management, so that I can one day get my own pony. How can I go about this?

A.   Looking after your own pony can be pretty hard work, so it is important before buying one, to find out whether you have sufficient knowledge and whether you would enjoy the day-to-day routine of looking after it. Getting wet, muddy and cold and tired can often make you reconsider! One of the best ways of finding out , and also of generally increasing your knowledge, is to ask at local riding schools if it would be possible to help at weekends and holidays. Some riding schools will give you an occasional lesson, or a small amount of pocket money for your hard work. This would give you a chance to improve your riding, but as this is not always the rule, don't expect it as your due. They will not necessarily be falling over themselves to get your assistance either, since an inexperienced helper can often create extra work for the staff. So be prepared to meet with a few negative responses. If you do succeed in becoming a weekend helper, you will have to be prepared to pull your weight if you want to stay.

Q. I'd like to try and get a holiday job at a trekking centre – how should I go about it?

A. At first this seems like a great way of getting a free holiday, but it is far less likely to work out so successfully. Working in a trekking centre can be hard, and does not mean that you are going to be included in the guests' social activities as a matter of course! Add to this the fact that many centres nowadays are also riding schools the whole year round, and so have their own qualified staff, and you will soon see that they are unlikely to welcome you with open arms!

If you are under sixteen years old, then you are not legally old enough to escort rides. If you are inexperienced they are highly unlikely to be interested. However, if you would like to try, are sixteen or over, and fairly competent, it might be worth asking, particularly the smaller centres. Write down all the details of your experience looking after horses and ponies, your

Fig. 51. Pony trekking.

standard of riding – be honest about it – and any other points which you feel are in your favour. Do be prepared for rejections, and don't expect more than your keep in return for help, with very possibly a small amount of pocket money.

Q.   I should like to set up a riding school when I leave school; are there any qualifications necessary to do this?

A.   You don't need qualifications as such if you are sufficiently experienced, but they can be very useful when it comes to attracting clients. To run a yard successfully, you will need some experience of a commercial establishment, so it might be worthwhile going on a working pupil training course studying towards your Assistant Instructors examination. Although such a course will be of a longer duration than if you trained as a fee-paying student, it does enable you to see more of the day to day running of a yard; and so would be of more practical benefit to you. You will need to be as businesslike as possible. It would be sensible to take a short typing course, and to learn about book-keeping and other aspects of running your own business. You might find a part-time or evening course running in your area if you make enquiries. If you prefer, some technical colleges run simultaneous A.I and typing/business studies type courses, but the drawback is that you do spend less time actually working with horses. The more experience you can gain, the better, and even after taking exams, you may still find it helpful to work in a small yard for someone else so that you learn as much as possible about all the ins and outs of it. Once you have decided to start your own school, you will need to apply for a licence from the local authorities, and to pass a yearly veterinary inspection.

Q.   I am interested in a career of some kind with horses when I leave school but as yet I am not sure whether I actually want to work with them, and if so in what capacity, or whether to settle for some related job. Are there any addresses I can write to which can send me information on what is involved in various lines of work, and what sort of training is needed?

A.   Working with horses involves long and anti-social hours of work, and is often badly paid in comparison to many other jobs; nevertheless, if you are sufficiently dedicated, you may well find it very rewarding work. The best way of finding out whether you would be suited to such a life would be to offer to help out at a local yard for a few weeks. Basic requirements of horses and ponies are the same regardless of the job they do and it would give you a better idea as to what you were letting yourself in for. Should you feel that working in a yard is not for you, but wish to take up some related occupation, there are still plenty of other options open, depending upon where your talents lie, and addresses you can write to for further information are given in chapter 16, pg 156.

Q. I am interested in training for a career with horses, and wonder whether there is any form of financial aid available?

A. It is very difficult to obtain any form of financial aid these days for work with horses, although there are one or two schemes, mainly aimed at school leavers. To find out what grants and schemes are operative in your particular area you should contact your County Education Office, or enquire at your local Job Centre. There are also a number of educational charities and foundations which are able to make small grants to students in special hardship or with special qualifications. Information on these can be obtained from the following publications:

The Annual Charities Register (can be consulted at most Reference Libraries)

The Educational Charities, published by the National Union of Students, 3 Endsleigh Street, London WC1

You might also consider working at a yard on a working pupil basis if you are thinking of taking up teaching as a career. Whilst fee-paying students receive more intensive instruction, and have only one or two horses to care for, a working pupil should receive around four or five lessons and lectures each week in return for providing labour. This usually involves caring for up to five horses and ponies, plus giving instruction to novice riders when you are considered ready. You will be expected to assist with all other stable duties also, and although the course is usually of a longer duration than a fee-paying student's (around six months to a year) it can in fact provide a more realistic education. You will be expected, however, to pay a small amount for your board and lodging unless you are close enough to live at home. Steer clear of yards which offer to pay 'pocket money' as these will not normally provide much instruction, and standards can sometimes be pretty low. Any yard which you think may be suitable should always be visited first of course, taking note of the appearance, condition of the horses, and standard of instruction. You should ask about what you can expect to receive in tuition, your duties and hours of work, time off, and so forth, and who will normally be teaching you. If possible, do have a chat with one or two of the working pupils already there so that you get a better idea of exactly what goes on.

Q.   I wonder if there are any exams I can take connected with horses? I do not wish to take up horses as a career, but as I am not very competitive, it would be nice to have some kind of goal.

A.   There are several exams which you can take; these are an excellent way of increasing your knowledge and gauging your amount of progress at the same time. A very popular series of exams are the ABRS Weekly Riders' Tests, graded from 1 – 10. These are divided into both riding and stable management sections, and can be taken at three-monthly intervals, but must be taken and passed in order, starting with 1. They are open to riders over the age of nine years old, who are regular riders at an ABRS approved riding school. The tests are reasonably cheap to take, and an application can be made through the school.

The BHS run a series of Horse Knowledge and Riding Stages exams graded from I – IV, although since recent revision, these are very much more geared now towards the professional hoping to make horses his or her career. These are divided into stable management and riding sections, but in order to gain a certificate, both sections have to be taken and passed. The minimum age at which the first exam may be taken is sixteen years, and it is advisable to seek some form of professional training before attempting them. Applications are made through the Training Office of the BHS.

A very practical exam to consider taking is the Riding and Road Safety exam, devised by the BHS in conjunction with Local Authorities. This is a three part test, divided into theory, simulated and actual, road tests. The minimum age to take this test is ten years old, the maximum, sixty five. You can apply to do so through your BHS County Road Safety Officer, and further details are contained in the BHS booklet 'Riding and Roadcraft'. If you belong to a Pony or Riding Club, you might like to attempt their graded exams. You should ask the Club's secretary about this, so that instructional rallies can be arranged in preparation for them.

14

Riding and Road Safety

Q. I need a new riding hat – but there seem to be so many available. I can't afford very much, so would a secondhand one be all right?

A. Never grudge spending money on sound head protection – lack of it could cost you your life. Probably the best protection is offered by a jockey skull cap; if you plan to ride in any cross country competitions you would certainly be advised to buy one, in fact you are unlikely to be allowed to compete unless you are wearing one. Pony Club members must also now wear skull caps in order to take part in their activities.

If you prefer the more traditional velvet or velveteen covered riding caps, do not let vanity override safety, always wear it with the chinstrap fastened. Whatever hat you choose, it must fit correctly. Different makes often have differently shaped crowns, so it is worth trying several on in the shop to find the best fit. This should be snug, although not so tight that it gives you a headache, and should sit squarely on your head rather than perched on the back like a fashion accessory, as is so frequently seen. If a drawlace is fitted, it should be tightened up a little so that there is an enclosed pocket of air between the hat and the top of the head, which in the event of a fall will provide a 'cushion'. Never buy an old hat, always invest in a new one which conforms to the latest BSI kitemark – BS6473 in the case of caps, and BS4472 for jockey skulls. You should buy from a saddler who displays a certificate showing that he has attended a hat fitting course, so that you get the best possible advice as to fit.

Q. Not long ago my horse was hit by a car. He has now recovered, and is quite sound, but has become very nervous in traffic. Is there anything that can be done to restore his confidence?

A. Horses and ponies have very good memories, and take a long time to forget unpleasant experiences. Although your horse may improve in time, there is no real guarantee. Grazing him in a field near to heavy traffic sometimes helps to overcome nervousness; but on the other hand there is the risk of being near to a major road should they escape, and actually riding amongst traffic is somewhat different. Try to avoid really congested areas, and never ride alone until you are confident in him again; even so you should still take the precaution of telling someone exactly where you intend to go, and how long you will be, before going out. You will find that the presence of

Fig. 52. Riding two abreast along a road.

another, steady, horse will help to give him a bit more confidence; where roads are broad enough and visibility ahead clear, you could keep this horse on your right hand side. Riding double like this will act as a barrier between you and the traffic, and enable you to keep both hands on the reins whilst your friend gives hand signals, it will encourage drivers to slow down and give you plenty of room when passing, too. If you are really worried about the situation and it looks as if your horse may become a real hazard on the roads both to yourself and to other people, then you may have to consider selling him, or else confining your activities to what can be done at home.

Q. Do I always have to ride along the left hand side of the road? Sometimes I feel my horse would be better off if he faced the traffic passing immediately by him, rather than having his back turned to it.

A.   You must always ride in the same direction as on-going traffic, and it is an offence to do otherwise. You must obey the Highway Code in the same way as other road users do, stopping for pedestrians at crossing points, and halting at red lights and so forth.

Q.   Which is the correct side to lead a horse from if riding and leading?

A.   If you have to ride and lead (which is never a good idea unless both animals are good in traffic, quiet with each other, and you have no other choice) then you should lead the horse from its off side. Put a bridle on, so that you have better control, and lead either by the reins, or by looping a lead rein through the bit rings. Keep the led horse's head up by your knee, and try to keep him well in to the side of the road, but with due regard for any pedestrians.

Q.   Is it all right to ride along grass verges?

A.   In some areas, grass verges seem to be almost the only places where it is possible to have a canter, or give the horse's legs a break from hard road surfaces. However, cantering along them is not very safe, since they often conceal hidden dangers such as tins, broken bottles, or drainage ditches. Added to this, should the horse shy at something in the hedge or fence, he will inevitably move sideways into the path of the traffic – which you may not be expecting him to do, and will therefore be in a bad position to try and prevent. Some counties do in fact ban horses from being ridden along verges, so it is as well to check up on this before doing so, otherwise you could end up with a fine. Certainly, it is illegal to ride or lead a horse or pony on the footway or pavement of urban streets.

Q.   My horse keeps shying at things in verges, and at drain covers. How can I stop him, as I am sure that a car will hit him one day when he is doing this?

A.   Some horses are very suspicious of anything which looks a bit odd – and if he has walked over a drain cover before, then the noise and sudden unexpected change in footing may have upset him. Nevertheless, you should get his eyesight checked by the vet, as poor vision could very well account for this habit.

Change your manner of tackling the problem too. Rather than using your left rein when you feel him beginning to spook, use your right leg and right rein to encourage him to bend away from the object. This will control his right shoulder and hindquarters, preventing him from swinging them into the middle of the road in an attempt to keep as far away as possible

Fig. 53.
(a) The wrong, and
(b) the correct way of keeping a horse at the side of the road.

from whatever it is that frightens him. Apply a similar principle when you hear a lorry or noisy vehicle approaching which might alarm him, as it will keep him close to the kerb, and likely to move closer towards it rather than into the path of the passing vehicle. He will also be able to see the vehicle as it approaches, out of his right eye; if he is on a left bend instead he is likely to resist your attempts to straighten him, and try to keep his left eye on the vehicle by swinging his quarters toward the centre of the road.

Q.   Which side of the road should I walk on when leading my horse along the road?

A.   You should lead him on the left hand side of the road, but from the off side so that you remain between him and any traffic. It is best to use a bridle for better control, and perhaps a pair of gloves too for better grip. You should take the reins over his head to lead him, unless he is wearing a martingale. In this case, you should either undo the martingale and lead him as described, or keep the reins around his neck, and take hold of them about four inches below the jaw.

Fig. 54. Leading in hand at the side of the road.

Q.   Although I don't actually ride in the dark, it is often getting a bit dull in the evening when I return home from a ride, and I worry in case a car driver should fail to see us.

A.   There are a number of products which can be used to make yourself more visible. Although fluorescent tabards are useful during the daytime, make sure that you buy one which has reflective material in it which will return light when it is shone on it. You could also put reflective leg bands on your horse's legs, and an armband on your right arm. Another very useful device is a stirrup light, which is like a small torch that can be attached to your stirrup iron. When leading at night, take the same precautions, and carry in your right hand a torch which shines white light to the front, and red light to the back.

15

Hunting

Q. I've never been hunting before, but I would quite like to now that I have my own horse. How do I find out which is my local Hunt? And do I have to be a member of it in order to hunt? If so, is it likely to be very expensive?

A. The weekly magazine 'Horse and Hound' publishes a special edition each year which carries a Hunt directory; or else you could find out which is your local Hunt by enquiring at riding or livery yards, or asking your Pony or Riding club. Once you have found out which Hunt is closest to you, contact its Secretary if you wish to join. It varies from one area to another as to whether you have to be a member in order to hunt – some Hunts insist that you are a member unless you have been invited as a guest, whilst others are more relaxed about it and don't mind casual visitors. Your Hunt Secretary will be able to tell you about this.

Hunting is an expensive sport though. In order to become a member you will be required to pay a yearly subscription, and in addition to this, each day that you hunt you will also be asked to pay 'field money'. If you are a visitor rather than a member you pay a 'cap' which varies from Hunt to Hunt – it may be as little as £25 or it could be considerably more. Subscriptions are payable each year on May 1st – although this is not the hunting season, it ensures that there are funds to support the packs and people who work for them throughout the summer months.

Q. I hope to go hunting soon – what should I wear? And will I have to carry a hunting whip – my horse is terrified of even a short crop, so I don't know what she would do if I have to carry one.

A. When cubhunting it is correct to wear a ratcatcher (tweed jacket). For hunting proper, what you wear depends rather upon who you are. A farmer wears an ordinary hunting cap, a gentleman subscriber wears a bowler (unless he has been invited to wear the Hunt button, when a top hat and red coat is in order). As safety is a topic very much to the fore these days, it is perfectly allowable though to wear a grey hunting cap instead, which is a great deal safer, if not as picturesque as the

Fig. 55. A hunt meeting.

traditional headgear. Ladies may wear either a bowler or hunting cap. The trend nowadays is more and more towards practicality, and since greater protection is offered by a skull cap, one of these may be worn if preferred, with a black silk or one of the velvet coverings which are now available. Both sexes should ideally wear a black jacket, excepting children, who should always wear a hacking jacket. A stock (more correctly called a hunting tie) should be worn with black jacket, long boots, spurs if desired, and beige jodhpurs. Children may wear a Pony Club or plain coloured tie, and should wear jodhpur boots rather than long boots. The ribbons on the backs of hard hats should be tucked up out of the way or cut off – only Hunt servants are allowed to let them hang down, as it is a means of distinguishing them from the rest of the field. A hunting

Fig. 56. Stages in the tying of a hunting tie.

whip is always an asset – very practical for opening and shutting gates – but they are expensive and a short stick is quite acceptable. Since your horse has a phobia about whips anyway, you would probably do better to manage without one at all. The most important point about your dress is to ensure that even if you only own a hacking jacket, your turnout is tidy and presentable; it is well worth the effort of plaiting your horse up, and most Hunts aren't too fussy provided you make an attempt to arrive at the Meet with both yourself and your horse looking well groomed. If you are in any doubt whatsoever about the suitability of your dress, contact the Hunt Secretary.

Q. How many times a week do hounds meet, and how can I find out where?

A.   Depending upon the area and numbers, Hunts may meet anywhere from two to five days a week. Dates are often advertised in the local press or in 'Horse and Hound'. In some areas Hunt saboteurs are active, so in these instances, dates and locations are often passed around by word of mouth, rather than published, but any Hunt member or the Hunt Secretary will be able to tell you.

Q. I am going hunting for the first time, but I am not sure what I should do on arriving at the Meet. I have read that I am supposed to greet the Master – are there any others I should make a point of meeting?

A.   Courtesy and tradition say that you should first of all greet the Master and wish him a good morning; but bearing in mind that you may not know who he is, or if there is a very large field with perhaps 200 people present, it is accepted that this isn't always practical. More importantly, ensure that your horse always stands facing the hounds – never allow him to turn his quarters towards them. If your horse kicks one, you might get sent home in disgrace before you have even started, and you definitely won't be popular! The Secretary or whoever is collecting field money and caps will usually notice you arriving, but otherwise you should seek them out and pay them. On seeing any Hunt Officials, it is of course, only polite to say 'good morning'. Always follow the Field Master and his instructions; if you need to find a gap in a hedge, or a gateway, be sure to follow the rules of the countryside and avoid damaging crops or disturbing livestock. Remember that the Hunt relies upon the goodwill of local landowners to allow them to continue meeting and hunting upon their land.

Q. What is the Hunt Supporters' Club? A friend mentioned something about it the other day, but it is the first I have heard about it.

A. Subscriptions to the Hunt have to cover major expenses, but each Hunt usually also has its own Supporters' Club. These clubs run all sorts of different events such as an annual Hunt Ball, point to points, and so forth, which help to raise funds for other expenses such as saddles and lorries. Most Hunt members, or the Secretary will be able to put you in touch with the Supporters' Club if you wish to join.

Q. I am unsure as to whether my tack is suitable for my horse when I take him hunting for the first time. I normally use a General Purpose saddle, jointed snaffle, and running martingale. Do I need a proper hunting saddle? And should I put boots or bandages on him? I feel that I ought to protect his legs if possible.

A. Your normal tack is fine, providing that it is safe and suitable for jumping and galloping in. Make a point of always checking it very carefully before hunting, for any weak points or rotting stitching. Places where leather comes into contact with metal are always vulnerable to wear and tear so these points should be thoroughly inspected. If your horse tends to become very strong when in the company of others, use a stronger bit; he will have other horses galloping both in front and beside him, which can prove every exciting for some animals, and it is essential to have good brakes. It is best not to use boots or bandages, as it is likely that you will be encountering some very wet and muddy going; after several hours with wet mud working its way between boots and skin your horse will become very uncomfortable. Bandages will quickly become wet and sodden too. When riding in a cross country competition, leg protection is quite sensible, but it is then worn for minutes rather than hours, and hunting is rather different.

Q.   I don't own a horse, and the local stables won't hire any out. However, my friend and I would like to follow the Hunt on foot if we can't do it any other way – are we likely to be told to go away?

A.   Lots of people gain a tremendous amount of pleasure and enjoyment from following on foot or in a car – some Hunts have a huge following like this. Some Hunts do also try and collect a small subscription from these followers, which is only fair really as followers are deriving enjoyment from the sport after all, and frequently causing problems like traffic jams, or causing exhaust fumes which can spoil the scent for hounds.

Q.   My friend is taking me hunting with her shortly; I know a little bit but not a great deal. I shall be joining her at the Meet – are there any special tips I should know about? I don't want to end up committing some terrible sin and embarrassing her!

A.   Be careful not to park your trailer or lorry at the Meet itself, but a reasonable distance away, otherwise problems can arise. If you are away for several hours, perhaps blocking someone in, they can't get out until you return! Also the area may become very congested with traffic. Try and find somewhere unobtrusive – not right in the middle of some poor farmer's gateway either. You might find that it is best to travel your horse already tacked up – it will save time and if your horse becomes excited when he hears the noise then it will also save you a lot of fuss.

Another tip to remember is that you should consider the fitness of your horse. It can be a very long day, one minute galloping, sometimes for quite long distances, the next standing around in the cold. It requires considerable stamina, and tires even a fairly fit horse more than you might realise. Your adrenalin will not keep your horse going. Turn for home when he begins to tire, as a weary horse is much more likely to make mistakes or to injure himself – better to save him and enjoy another day's hunting on him in the future.

Q.   The last time I went hunting with the Pony Club, my pony was fine whilst we were standing still, but every time we moved off he got really strong, and was difficult to hold. His last owner hunted him a couple of times and didn't have any trouble stopping him – should I persevere with a snaffle, which I normally ride in, or change to a pelham? And should I use two pairs of reins with it if I do?

A.   When a horse or pony has been hunted a few times, it begins to anticipate what is going to happen, and not surprisingly, will often get excited. It sounds as though this is what has happened with your pony, coupled with the fact that perhaps his previous owner was a bit stronger than you. A change to a pelham when he is hunting sounds like a good idea, so that he has a little more respect for you. Two pairs of reins are more correct on a pelham, so that you can achieve either a snaffle or a curb type action on his mouth and head, but if you find it all a bit of a handful to manage, it would be best to use one pair of reins attached to pelham roundings. Do check the roundings carefully for safety, as they have to put up with a lot of wear, and are only made of leather.

Q.   I'd like to take my horse hunting as I feel it would be good experience for him, but I'm not sure that I like the idea of a fox possibly getting killed at the end of it. Is there an alternative?

A.   You might try draghunting, which is similar to proper hunting in that hounds and hunt staff are present, but instead of chasing a fox, hounds follow an artificial scent which has previously been laid over a specially prepared line of country. It can be quite exciting as you are guaranteed a fast run with plenty of fences to jump. You can find out when the next draghunt is being held in your area by looking it up in 'Horse and Hound'.

Q.   Are there any special things I should do for my horse when he comes back from hunting?

A.   The care of a horse after hunting (or indeed a cross country event) is just as important as the preparation beforehand. Once you return home, check him over very carefully for any cuts, scrapes, or thorns which may have become embedded in the legs. You can find the latter by running your fingers gently upwards against the lie of the hair; should you find one, trim the hair away from the area, withdraw with a pair of tweezers, and poultice. All cuts, however trivial they may seem, should be dealt with promptly, since neglecting them could allow an infection to build up which will put the horse off work for some time. Check also for overreaches – cuts in the heels of the front feet – since these are sometimes concealed by a flap of skin. It is best not to wash off muddy legs unless treatment for an injury is required, but rather to let them dry naturally, after which the mud can be brushed off. Washing tends to work dirt into the pores of the skin, which often remain open for some time when the horse is tired, and this could set up a nasty infection.

If the horse is to remain stabled for the night, then put a set of stable bandages on which will help to support tired legs and ensure that he is warm enough (a tired horse is less able to create as much body heat). Remove the worst of the mud and sweat, but don't make too much of a fuss – just do enough to make him comfortable for the night. Put yourself in the same position; after a strenuous day quite often all you feel like doing is sitting down and putting your feet up with a bit of peace and quiet.

Rather than giving him his normal feed, give a bran mash instead which will have a laxative effect and ensure that his digestive system does not seize up through tiredness. Add a double handful of glucose to it as well as Epsom salts, as this will make it both more palatable, and help perk him up a bit so that he feels the effects of tiredness less. If he is to be turned out for the night, make sure that he is dry first, as a wet coat in cold weather will lead to him getting chilled. If he is able to stay in, put a sweat rug on beneath his normal rugs in case he 'breaks out' and starts sweating again during the evening. This sometimes happens if the horse has an excitable nature, or if he is very tired and the skin pores take a long time to start functioning properly again. You should check him later in the evening to make sure that he is comfortable and there are no further problems. The next day, he will probably appreciate a day off, and should be either turned out, led out in hand, or ridden out in walk for half an hour so that he has a chance to stretch his legs and loosen off any stiffness.

16

What to Join and Useful Addresses

(Note. All the names and addresses given here are correct at the time of going to press, but are bound to change and become progressively more out-of-date as time passes.)

Q. I have been on a few sponsored rides over varying distances, from twelve to twenty miles, and I have enjoyed the challenge of getting my horse fit for them. I would now like to try some more competitive long rides. Is there a society which runs such rides, and would it be possible for my daughter to join as well – she is only twelve, but seems to cope very well?

A. The BHS Long Distance Group organise a number of different rides ranging from Pleasure Rides of fifteen miles upwards, Qualifying Rides of between thirty and forty miles, and Major Rides of approximately fifty to one hundred miles. In order to compete in them, you need to be a member of the BHS and of the Long Distance Group, details of which are available from the BHS, British Equestrian Centre, Stoneleigh, Kenilworth, Warwicks CV8 2LR. If you wish to try some long distance rides with your daughter however, you might prefer to join the Endurance Horse and Pony Society which runs rides throughout the country from Devon to Scotland, ranging in distances from a twenty mile minimum novice ride to an annual one hundred mile ride. They are fairly informal, and juniors are as welcome as adults, and it is not even necessary to be a member in order to participate in the rides. Details of rides and membership are available from Endurance Horse and Pony Society of GB, 15 Newport Drive, Alcester, Warwickshire.

Q. My horse is going well in Open classes in local jumping shows, and I would like to affiliate her for BSJA competitions. Where do I apply?

A. You should write to the British Showjumping Association, British Equestrian Centre, Stoneleigh, Kenilworth, Warwicks CV8 2LR.

*Q.   I have just moved to a new area where I am able at last to
buy and keep a horse. I should very much like to meet other
horsy people in the area – how do I go about this?*

A.   Your best move is probably to join a Riding Club or Saddle
Club (these latter are unaffiliated). These not only organise local
shows, but all sorts of other events too, ranging from instructional rallies to social gatherings. You should be able to discover
where your local clubs are by asking at nearby riding or livery
stables, or else you could ring or write to the BHS to find out
which is your nearest affiliated Riding Club. The address is:
British Horse Society, British Equestrian Centre, Stoneleigh,
Kenilworth, Warwickshire CV8 2LR. Tel: (0203) 696697. If
you are a junior, you might consider joining the Pony Club; if
you cannot find out which is your local branch, then you should
once again write to the BHS.

*Q.   I pass a field every day which has some ponies living in it.
The field is very bare with little or no grass on it, and I have
never seen them being fed. Often the water tank is empty and
the ponies themselves look very thin and neglected. Whom should
I contact about them?*

A.   Get in touch with your local BHS Welfare Officer – you
can find out who this is if you are not sure by either contacting
your local BHS County Committee, or ringing the BHS on
(0203) 696697. You could also contact the International League
for the Protection of Horses (see below).

*Q.   I would like to help sponsor a horse or pony in some way
as I cannot afford either financially or in terms of time, to support
one of my own full time. Is there a charity which runs such a
scheme?*

A.   There are a number of equine charities which do indeed
run such schemes. Many of these charities rely entirely upon
voluntary donations, and even a small contribution will be wel-
comed:
Home of Rest for Horses, Westcroft Stables, Speen Farm, nr
Aylesbury, Bucks
International League for the Protection of Horses, Overa House
Farm, Larling, Norwich, Norfolk NR16 2QX. Tel: (0953)
717882/717309.
HAPPA, 64 Station Road, Padiham, Lancs BB12 8EF

Ada Cole Memorial Stables, Broadlands, Broadley Common, nr Nazeing, Waltham Abbey, Essex EN9 2DH
Brooke Hospital for Animals, Cairo, Dept HR, 1 Regent Street, London SW1Y 4PA
Tettenhall Horse Sanctuary Foundation, South Perton Farm, Jenny Walkers Lane, Wolverhampton WV6 7HB
Lluest Horse and Pony Trust, 48 Court Orchard Lodge, Wotton under Edge, Glos
The Donkey Sanctuary, Slade House, Salcombe Regis, Sidmouth, Devon

Useful Addresses
Breed Societies and Associations

Arab Horse Society, Windsor House, Ramsbury, Marlborough, Wilts SN8 2PE
British Andalusian Horse Society, Rohanber, Gull Lane, Framingham Pigot, Norwich, Norfolk.
British Appaloosa Society, 2 Frederick Street, Rugby, Warwickshire CV21 2EN
British Lipizzaner Horse Society, Ausdan Stud, Glynarthen, Llandysul, Dyfed SA44 6PB
British Morgan Horse Society, George and Dragon Hall, Mary Place, London W11 4PL
British Mule Society, Hope Mount Farm, Top of Hope, Alstonfield, Ashbourne, Derbyshire DE6 2FR
British Palomino Society, Penrhiwllan, Llandysul, Dyfed SA44 5NZ
British Percheron Horse Society, Buttsbury Lodge, Stock Road, Stock, Ingatestone, Essex CM4 9PJ
British Quarter Horse Association, 4th Street, National Agricultural Centre, Stoneleigh, Warwickshire CV8 2LG
British Show Hack, Cob and Riding Horse Association, Rookwood, Packington Park, Meriden, Warwickshire
British Show Pony Society, 124 Green End Road, Sawtry, Huntingdon, Cambs PE17 5XA
British Skewbald and Piebald Association, West Fen House, High Road, Little Downham, Ely, Cambs CB6 2TB
British Spotted Pony Society, Weston Manor, Corscombe, Dorchester, Dorset DT2 0PB
British Trakhener Association, 230 Staines Road, Twickenham, Middlesex TW2 5AR
Coloured Horse and Pony Society, 15 Wilga Road, Welwyn, Herts AL6 9PT

Connemara Pony Breeders Society, 73 Dalysfort Road, Salthill, Galway, Eire

Cleveland Bay Horse Society, York Livestock Centre, Murton, York YO1 3UF

Dales Pony Society, 196 Springvale Road, Walkley, Sheffield S6 3NU

Dartmoor Pony Society, Whitethorne Cottage, Hittisleigh, Exeter EX6 6LG

Donkey Breed Society, Manor Cottage, South Thoresby, Alford, Lincs LN13 0AS

English Connemara Pony Society, 2 The Leys, Salford, Chipping Norton, Oxon OX7 5FD

Exmoor Pony Society, Glen Fern, Waddicombe, Dulverton, Somerset TA22 9RY

Falabella Breed Society, Kilverstone Wildlife Park, Thetford, Norfolk.

Fell Pony Society, Greylads Cottage, Larriston Farm, Newcastleton, Roxburgh TD9 0SL

Fjord Horse Society of GB, Ausdan Stud, Glynarthern, Llandysul, Dyfed SA44 6PB

Hackney Horse Society, Clump Cottage, Chitterne, Warminster, Wilts BA12 0LL

Haflinger Society of GB, Silverhill, 482 Market Street, Whitworth, Rochdale, Lancs

Highland Pony Society, Beechwood, Elie, Fife KY9 1DH

Icelandic Horse Society of GB, Rosebank, Higher Merley Lane, Corfe Mullen, Dorset BH21 3EG

Irish Draught Horse Society (GB), 4th Street, National Agricultural Centre, Stoneleigh, Warwickshire CV8 2LG

National Pony Society, Brook House, 25 High Street, Alton, Hants GU34 1AW

New Forest Pony and Cattle Breeding Society, Beacon Cottage, Burley, Ringwood, Hants BH24 4EH

Ponies Association (UK), Chesham House, 56 Green End Road, Sawtry, Huntingdon, Cambs PE17 5UY

Shetland Pony Stud Book Society, Pedigree House, 6 Kings Place, Perth PH2 8AD

Shire Horse Society, East of England Showground, Peterborough PE2 0XE

Suffolk Horse Society, The Market Hill, Woodbridge, Suffolk IP12 4LU

Welsh Pony and Cob Society, 6 Chalybeate Street, Aberystwyth, Dyfed SY23 1HS

Special Interest Clubs and Societies

British Driving Society, 27 Dugard Place, Barford, nr. Warwick CV35 8DX

British Field Sports Society, 59 Kennington Road, London SE1 7PZ

British Horse Society, British Equestrian Centre, Stoneleigh, Kenilworth, Warwickshire CV8 2LR

British Show Jumping Association, British Equestrian Centre, Stoneleigh, Kenilworth, Warwickshire CV8 2LR

British Vaulting Association, Gwanas Fawr, Dolgellau, Gwynedd

Endurance Horse and Pony Society of GB, 15 Newport Drive, Alcester, Warks

Equine Behaviour Study Circle, Grove Cottage, Brinkley, Newmarket, Suffolk CB8 0SF

Horse and Pony Model Club, 37 Finch Close, The Parks, Tadley, Hants RG2 6YJ

Horse Rangers Association, Royal Mews, Hampton Court Palace, East Molesey, Surrey KT8 9BW

Model Horses Unlimited, 5 Brington Road, Long Buckby, Northants NN6 7RW

Mounted Games Association of GB, Bunces Farm, Runwick, Farnham, Surrey GU10 5EP

Riding for the Disabled Association, National Agricultural Centre, Stoneleigh, Kenilworth, Warks CV8 2LY

Side Saddle Association, Highbury House, 19 High Street, Welford, Northants NN6 7HT

Western Equestrian Society, Hillview Cottage, Windmill Lane, Ladbroke, Leamington Spa, Warks CV33 0BN

Western Horseman's Association of GB, 13 East View, Barnet, Herts EN5 5TL

Careers – Useful Addresses

Association of British Riding Schools, Old Brewery Yard, Penzance, Cornwall TR18 2SL

British Horse Society, British Equestrian Centre, Stoneleigh, Kenilworth, Warwickshire CV8 2LR

British Racing School, Snailwell Road, Newmarket, Suffolk

Cordwainers Technical College, 182 Mare Street, Hackney, London E8 3RE

Royal College of Veterinary Surgeons, 32 Belgrave Square, London SW1X 8QP

Society of Master Saddlers, The Cottage, 4 Chapel Place, Mary Street, Bovey Tracey, Devon TQ13 9JA

Worshipful Company of Farriers, The Old Granary, High Street, Barcombe Cross, nr. Lewes, East Sussex BN8 5DH

Security Marking

Equestrian Security Services, 17 St Johns Road, Farnham, Surrey GU9 8NU

'Identichip', Animal Care Ltd, Common Road, Dunnington, York YO1 5RU

MMB Farmkey, 28 West Bar, Banbury, Oxon OX16 9RR

Index

FREE

If you would like an up-to-date list of all **RIGHT WAY** titles currently available, please send a stamped self-addressed envelope to

ELLIOT RIGHT WAY BOOKS
KINGSWOOD, SURREY, KT20 6TD, U.K.